Elementary VI

D1308522

Know Your
Bible

By Mary Alice Jones

Illustrated by Seymour Fleishman

RAND McNALLY & COMPANY

Chicago · New York · San Francisco

Copyright © 1965 by Rand McNally & Company
Copyright 1965 under International Copyright Union by Rand McNally & Company
All rights reserved.   Printed in U.S.A.
Library of Congress Catalog Card Number: 64–17447
First printing, October, 1965
Second printing, September, 1966

Acknowledgments

Grateful acknowledgment is made to the following for
the photographs used in this book:

AMERICAN BIBLE SOCIETY, for the drawing on p. 63.

AMERICAN SCHOOL OF ORIENTAL RESEARCH, for the photo on p. 53.

THE BETTMAN ARCHIVE, INC., for the photo on p. 35.

THE BRITISH MUSEUM, for the three photos on p. 20.

THE BROOKLYN MUSEUM, for the photos on p. 49.

COWMAN PUBLISHING COMPANY, for the drawing on p. 9 from *A Layman's Guide
to the Bible,* by Donald E. Demaray.

THE MATSON PHOTO SERVICE, for the photos on pp. 14, 16, 31, 32, 47, 48, 54, 66, 68, and 69.

J. LANE MILLER, for the photo on p. 33.

ORIENTAL INSTITUTE, the University of Chicago, for the photo on p. 22.

NATIONAL COUNCIL OF THE CHURCHES of Christ, for the photo on p. 62.

PALESTINE ARCHAEOLOGICAL MUSEUM, for the photos on p. 70 (a and c)

RYLANDS LIBRARY, for the photos on pp. 6, 9, 54 (a), 57, 59, and 60.

E. L. SUKENIK, for the photo on p. 70 (b).

Unless otherwise noted, the Bible quotations in the text
are from the Revised Standard Version, copyright 1946 and 1952.

The maps on pages 13, 30, 34, and 67 are adapted from
THE BIBLE ATLAS, by Emil G. Kraeling, copyright 1962 by Rand McNally & Company.

Table of Contents

Maps and Charts

All flesh is like grass
and all its beauty like the flower
of the field.
The grass withers, the flower fades;
but the word of our God
will stand forever.

Isaiah 40:6,8

What Is the Bible?

EVERY day in countries all over the world and in many languages thousands of copies of the Bible are bought. This has been true year after year after year, for hundreds of years. The Bible is not a book which is a "best seller" for a few months and then is forgotten. It has been read and cherished down through the centuries. It is read and cherished today. More people have read the Bible than have read any other book ever written.

The Bible you read is in English, but the Bible was not first written in English. The words which we read in English were first put into writing in ancient languages, long, long before there was an English language. All the Bibles in English and in French and German and Italian and Spanish and Japanese and Chinese and all the other languages men speak today are translations of ancient manuscripts.

Through the years scholars of many different countries have worked to find and translate these ancient copies of the Bible. Protestant scholars and Roman Catholic scholars and Jewish scholars from all around the world are sharing their findings and their knowledge and their skill. And so more and more is being learned every year about the Bible and what it says and what its words mean.

What is this book which has been translated into so many languages and on which so many scholars have worked so hard? Why has it been so greatly treasured by people of all conditions throughout the centuries? Why is this book from ancient times so important in our modern world? What is it about? Where did it come from? Who wrote it? How has it been preserved throughout the generations?

To begin, let us look at the Bible as we know it today.

When you hold in your hands a copy of the Bible as it is usually published today it is a rather large book. It would be even larger if it were not almost always printed on light-weight paper. Unless very fine print is used, most copies of the Bible today have over a thousand pages of text.

The Bible as a Book

The Bible is one book in the sense that its contents are now usually bound within one cover. It looks like one book. But actually it is many books brought together.

It is one book in the sense that it has one subject, one great theme throughout all its books. Yet within the books of the Bible this theme is treated in many different ways.

The Books in the Bible

The books in the Bible are all about God and what he did and how men responded to him. They were all written to show what God is like and what he calls man to be and to do. But the books were written in times which differed from one another, when the daily needs of the people were different, when the conditions under which they lived were different. Some books were put into writing at times when man's understanding of God was limited, and some were written when it was broad and deep. Some show men's primitive ideas of how they thought God wanted his children to worship him; others express noble thoughts of worship. And so the books differ in their purposes and reasons for their being written. This gives each book a flavor which is different from the others, and an atmosphere of its own. Some of the books are full of activity, vigorous, rapid-moving, written as if set down quickly. Others are quiet, meditative, beautiful in language and thought and form.

The books now included in the Bible were put into writing by many different persons. The writing was done during a long, long period in history, exactly how long no one knows for sure. The writers used different languages. They wrote in countries as different as ancient Israel and ancient Babylon and ancient Rome. They lived under different types of rulers and different forms of government and followed different manners and customs.

Some of the writers wrote poetry. Some of them wrote stories and parables. Some of them wrote the history of kings and nations. Some of them wrote the lives of great men and women. Some of them wrote sermons. Some of them wrote wise sayings called proverbs. Some of them wrote letters.

Ancient languages in which the Bible, or portions of it, was copied. (a) A fragment from Matthew in Coptic; (b) a fragment from the Old Testament in Hebrew; (c) a fragment in Syriac.

(a)   (b)   (c)

THE BOOKS OF THE BIBLE

Old Testament

GENESIS	I KINGS	ECCLESIASTES	OBADIAH
EXODUS	II KINGS	SONG OF SOLOMON	JONAH
LEVITICUS	I CHRONICLES	ISAIAH	MICAH
NUMBERS	II CHRONICLES	JEREMIAH	NAHUM
DEUTERONOMY	EZRA	LAMENTATIONS	HABAKKUK
JOSHUA	NEHEMIAH	EZEKIEL	ZEPHANIAH
JUDGES	ESTHER	DANIEL	HAGGAI
RUTH	JOB	HOSEA	ZECHARIAH
I SAMUEL	PSALMS	JOEL	MALACHI
II SAMUEL	PROVERBS	AMOS	

New Testament

MATTHEW	I CORINTHIANS	II THESSALONIANS	I PETER
MARK	II CORINTHIANS	I TIMOTHY	II PETER
LUKE	GALATIANS	II TIMOTHY	I JOHN
JOHN	EPHESIANS	TITUS	II JOHN
ACTS OF THE APOSTLES	PHILIPPIANS	PHILEMON	III JOHN
	COLOSSIANS	HEBREWS	JUDE
ROMANS	I THESSALONIANS	JAMES	REVELATION

Apochrypha

Although not included in the canon of the Scriptures, these books throw light upon the Bible. In some versions of the Bible they are bound in, usually between the Old Testament and the New Testament. They were not a part of the Hebrew text of the Old Testament but were included in the first translation of the Greek Septuagint Version of the Old Testament. They were copied into early Latin translations. They are a special sort of library of ancient sacred books.

ESDRAS	WISDOM OF SOLOMON	BEL AND THE DRAGON
TOBIT	ECCLESIASTICUS	I AND II MACCABEES
JUDITH	BARUCH	
ESTHER (*additions to the book in the Old Testament*)	SONG OF THE THREE CHILDREN	

The Two Testaments

In the Bible used by Christians today these books are grouped in two parts.

The *Old Testament* is the part that tells about what happened from the creation of the world to the time when Jesus Christ was born. This is the Bible of the Jewish people today. There are thirty-nine books in the Old Testament of today.

The *New Testament* tells about what happened beginning with the birth of Jesus and continuing through the time of the early Christian church. There is a final chapter about the future. In the New Testament there are twenty-seven books.

The word "Testament" is a translation of an ancient word which means a covenant or solemn agreement. The Old Testament is called "old" because it tells about the covenant God made with his people early in their history. The New Testament is called "new" because it tells about the covenant God made with his people later in history when Jesus Christ came to live among men.

The Making of the Canon

The story of how all the books of the Old Testament and all the books of the New Testament (and only these books) came together to form the Bible as it is today is a long story. It is called "making the canon."

The word "canon" means the list or collection of books which are received as sacred writings inspired of God, or Scripture. It was a long, long time—thousands of years—from the first writing of the first words that became a part of the Bible to the time when the canon was closed. The people of God, those who believed in God and sought to know his will and to obey his law, were convinced that some writings were inspired of God. That is, they were written by men especially called of God, especially responsive to God. Though some other writings were considered helpful, only those which were accepted through the years by the people of God as being inspired by God were put into the canon.

Besides the books included in the canon of the Old Testament and of the New Testament, there are some other ancient religious writings called the *Apocrypha* which form a special library. In some modern editions of the Bible these books are bound with the Old Testament or in between the Old Testament and the New Testament.

How the Bible Got Its Name

The word "Bible" comes from Greek by way of Latin, as do many words in the English language. It is an interesting fact that the Bible got its name not from its contents but from the material on which it was written. In the early days, this material often was made from a grass called papyrus, which was put together in long strips. After the writing was done on the strips, they were rolled around rods for convenience in handling. A papyrus roll was called a *biblion*. The plural was used to mean more than one roll and this word became *Bible*. Actually, then, Bible means "the papyrus rolls" or "the books." The use of the word Bible to refer to sacred writings of the canon goes back more than fifteen hundred years to about the year 400 A.D.

Now that we have looked at the Bible as a book which we can hold in our hands, let us think of the important questions, "What is the Bible about?" "Why is it so important to so many men today?"

What the Bible Is About

The Bible is about God. It is called the Word of God. That is, men believe that through the Bible God himself speaks to men today. The Bible tells about what God has done and about

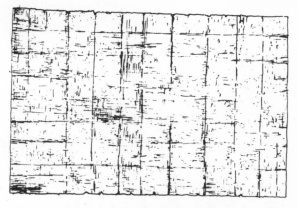

A pen sketch of papyrus writing material, showing the vertical and horizontal lines.

The oldest manuscript portion of the New Testament known to exist—a Greek papyrus fragment from the first half of the second century A.D.

how God has made himself known to men and nations from generation to generation.

In the opening words of the Bible, we read, "In the beginning, God ..." The last book in the Bible, in the last chapter, says God is "the first and the last, the beginning and the end." And the book nearest the middle of the Bible declares, "From everlasting to everlasting, thou art God." Thus from the first book to the last, the Bible is about God.

It is because the Bible is about God and how God expresses his love and concern for his children that people know it is important to them. It helps them answer questions which they are always asking. Questions like, "How did everything begin?" "How can one individual person be important in the whole universe?" "How do people know what is right and what is wrong?" "What is God like?" "How do we know God cares about per-

sons?" "What is going to happen to me when I die?" "Why do people suffer?" "Why is there evil in the world?" "How can I be happy?"

People read and cherish the Bible because it helps to answer their important questions. It answers them by telling about God' and his good purposes for his children.

An old Indian chief said of the Bible, "I know this book is the word of God because it pulls my heart."

The Theme of the Bible

The sacred books brought together in the Bible give an account of God's acts and man's response to God. It is a long story, including many nations and peoples, some good and some bad. But it has one central theme.

The story begins with God's mighty acts in creating the world. It tells how amid his mighty acts, God planned one creature for companionship with himself. Man was called to love and worship God, to talk with God and to work with God.

But the Bible tells how man chose to follow his own desires rather than to trust God, to talk with God, and listen to God. Because man separated himself from God, his creator, sin and suffering and loneliness and fear came into the world.

The rest of the Bible tells how through the generations God sought to save men from this sin and loneliness and to win them to be his loving children, responsive to his good purposes for them so their lives could be blessed as God had planned for them to be. It tells how God's steadfast love for men never failed and stopped at nothing to win men to himself.

This is the theme that runs through all the books of the Bible—God's good purposes for his children, man's sin, God's righteous judgment on sin, and his seeking, steadfast, suffering love to win men from their sin to fellowship with himself and a life of love for others. And the Bible promises that God's purposes will triumph.

God in the Bible

In the beginning, God created the heavens and the earth.

GENESIS 1:1

From everlasting to everlasting, thou art God.

PSALMS 90:2

I am the Alpha and Omega, the first and the last, the beginning and the end.

REVELATION 22:13

God Speaks to Man

Hear, O Israel: The Lord our God is one Lord, and you shall love the Lord your God with all your heart, and with all your soul, and with all your might. And these words which I command you this day shall be upon your heart; and you shall teach them diligently to your children, and shall talk of them when you sit in your house, and when you walk by the way, and when you lie down, and when you rise.

DEUTERONOMY 6:4-7

In many and various ways God spoke of old to our fathers by the prophets; but in these last days he has spoken to us by a Son. . . .

HEBREWS 1:1-2a

The Story the Old Testament Tells

"IN the beginning God created the heavens and the earth. And the earth was without form and void, and darkness was upon the face of the deep; and the Spirit of God was moving over the face of the waters."

Thus the Old Testament begins with the statement of faith that all that is began in the thought and purpose of God. In a glorious hymn of praise, it goes on to picture the creation of light, the sky and sea and dry land; the sun and moon and stars; plants and trees; fish and birds, and living creatures upon the earth. And to affirm God's plan that all living creatures be fruitful and multiply.

There are many ancient accounts of the beginning of all things. But the Bible account is different from the others. In many of the other accounts the gods were a part of creation; in the Bible account, God was the cause of all creation. All that was created depended upon God, and God was not dependent upon anything else. God's creation had purpose, as well.

It was moving always toward something grander and more wonderful. It was good.

Man's Special Gifts

But the most wonderful part of creation was yet to come. In the purpose of God there was to be man, a creature who could think God's thought after him, who could plan and act. In the good purpose of God, man was to have companionship with God himself, to enter into God's purposes, to work with God to make the world beautiful and fruitful and good.

Thus the Bible affirms the faith that God was the creator of all things, and that in the purpose of God, man was to have a special place, to respond to God as a person.

But in order to be a person, man had to be able to choose. So God gave man the gift of choosing. The sun and moon and stars, the sea and the mountains follow God's plan, but they do not choose. Only man may choose.

The Beginning of Sin

The Bible story goes on to tell how man misused his great gift of freedom to choose. He chose not to seek to know and follow God's good plan. In the story of Adam and Eve in the garden of Eden the Bible tells how man chose to try to hide from God and follow his own selfish desires instead of trusting God. The story says that because Adam and Eve turned their backs on God and his goodness, sin and suffering came into man's life. The creature who, in the purpose of God, was to be closest to God, to share the thoughts of God, thus separated himself from God.

But God did not take away from man the freedom to choose. Only by having freedom to choose could man ever really be what God planned for him to be, a person. So the Bible from this point on tells how God sought to win man to choose to be what God planned for him to be.

Through the lives of individual men and women and of nations, the Bible continues the story of what God did and how man responded to him.

In the story of Noah, the Bible tells of the sin of the people and of a great flood which threatened to destroy all life on the earth. But Noah was a righteous man who walked with God. He and his family and a pair of each kind of animal were saved in a large ark, or boat, which rode out the flood. When the flood receded and Noah and his family and the animals came out of the ark, the sun shone again. And there in the sky was a beautiful rainbow. As

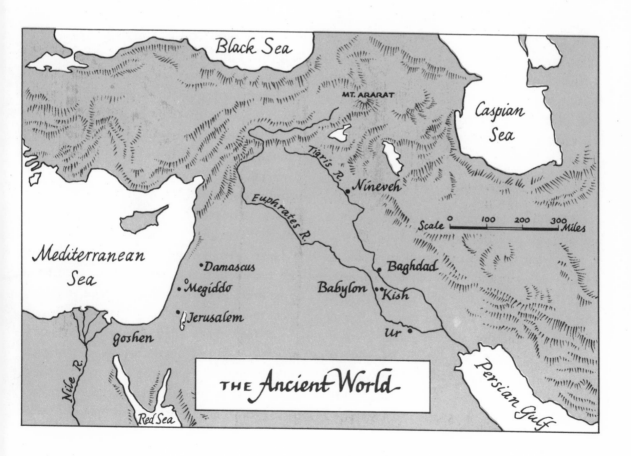

Excavation of ruins at Ur. Here Abraham lived before he set out for the Land of Canaan.

Noah and his family worshiped God, God made himself known to them through the bow in the sky.

Noah's sons, Shem and Ham and Japeth, became the fathers and grandfathers of many peoples. And so, generation after generation, the population of the world increased.

A People Chosen by God

Now the Bible tells how God chose a family and a people to be his people in a special way, to hear what God was saying to man, and to follow God's way and teach it to their children.

Abraham was the first of the great leaders called "patriarchs." The word means father or leader of a family or tribe. Abraham lived in the city of Ur near the great river Euphrates. But Ur was a pagan city and her people worshiped the moon goddess. So God called Abraham to leave Ur and go to a new country, and

to rear his family to worship God. The Bible story tells how God was with Abraham as he and his family journeyed to the Land of Canaan, which was to be their homeland. And God said to Abraham, "Walk before me and I will make my covenant between me and you and I will make nations of you, and kings shall come forth from you. And I will establish my covenant between me and you and your descendents after you."

Isaac, Abraham's son, and then Jacob, his grandson, became patriarchs after him.

These were primitive times, and even the best men followed customs which seem to us to be cruel. But the patriarchs were very clear about one thing. They knew they were the people of God. They knew they were dependent upon God. They trusted God and taught their children and all their people to worship God. Jacob came to be called Israel, and thereafter these people were called "the people of Israel."

EAST UNITED METHODIST
CHILDREN'

The Story of Joseph

Jacob had twelve sons. Joseph was the one who seems to have been the ablest. He dreamed wonderful dreams of the future. He seems to have been his father's favorite, though he was next to the youngest son, and because of this, his older brothers were jealous of him. One day when the brothers were away from home with their father's flocks, they saw a caravan coming, on the way to Egypt. The older brothers decided that this offered an opportunity to get rid of the young dreamer. They sold Joseph to the merchants, and he was taken to Egypt.

Though he began his life in Egypt as a slave, through hard work and dependence upon God, Joseph became a powerful man in Egypt. During time of plenty when the crops were bountiful he stored the surplus grain. Then when famine came he had the grain to feed the people. He kept the people of Egypt alive and was honored next to Pharaoh the king.

The famine spread to Canaan and the family of Joseph's father, Jacob, was in need. The father sent his sons to Egypt to buy grain. When they came before Joseph, he knew them at once. But they did not recognize in the powerful officer the younger brother whom they had wronged. Joseph made himself known to them and forgave them. He told them that though they had done evil, God had used it for good and enabled him to preserve life. Then he sent for his father and all his relatives. Thus the children of Israel moved from Canaan to Egypt and prospered there.

Slavery and Deliverance

As the generations passed, new Pharaohs came to the throne of Egypt. Both they and the peo-

A sunrise view over the Wilderness of Judaea, the Dead Sea, and the Mountains of Moab.

ple forgot all that Joseph had done for their fathers in saving their country from famine. They saw the foreign Israelites settling on some of the best land in the country. The Egyptians began to oppress the Israelites. They finally made them slaves, working hard under harsh overseers.

But God did not forget his promise to Abraham. He did not forget his people.

God called Moses to be a new leader of the people of Israel. God promised, "Certainly I will be with you." The Bible story tells how God enabled Moses to lead the children of Israel out of Egypt and across the Red Sea. It tells of the long, hard journey across the wilderness back toward Canaan, the land of their fathers, Abraham, Isaac, and Jacob. It tells how the people suffered and so rebelled against Moses and against God himself. It tells how God provided food and water for the rebellious people and led them on.

The Covenant at Mt. Sinai

The Bible tells about the covenant God made with the people at Mount Sinai. It tells of the giving of God's law to the people through Moses. The Ten Commandments summarize this law.

Mt. Sinai where, according to tradition, Moses received the Ten Commandments.

>>>->>>->>>->>>->>> # THE TEN COMMANDMENTS <<<-<<<-<<<-<<<-<<<

And God spoke all these words, saying,

I am the Lord Your God, who brought you out of the Land of Egypt, out of the house of bondage.

You shall have no other gods before me.

You shall not make yourself a graven image. . . .

You shall not take the name of the Lord your God in vain; for the Lord will not hold him guiltless who takes his name in vain.

Remember the sabbath day, to keep it holy. Six days you shall labor, and do all your work; but the seventh day is a sabbath to the Lord your God; in it you shall not do any work, you, or your son, or your daughter, or your manservant, or your maidservant, or your cattle, or the sojourner who is within your gates; . . .

Honor your father and your mother, that your days may be long in the land which the Lord your God gives you.

You shall not kill.

You shall not commit adultery.

You shall not steal.

You shall not bear false witness against your neighbor.

You shall not covet your neighbor's house; you shall not covet your neighbor's wife, or his manservant, or his maidservant, or his ox, or his ass, or anything that is your neighbor's.

EXODUS 20:1-4; 7, 8-10a; 12-17

The story goes on. Moses died on the threshold of the promised land toward which the children of Israel had been journeying so long. Joshua succeeded Moses as leader. He had a hard job ahead of him. God promised to be with Joshua as he had been with Moses. "Be strong and of good courage; be not frightened, neither be dismayed; for the Lord your God is with you." This promise made all the difference. And thus under Joshua, the people of Israel re-entered their homeland.

The Time of the Judges

After the death of Joshua, a succession of leaders arose. They were called "judges," but they were primarily warriors, for the conquest of Canaan required many years of fighting. The most famous of the judges was Gideon, the hero warrior, who won a great victory with a handful of men and unwarlike weapons. His story is told in Judges 6, 7, and 8.

These were rough times, with little central

authority, when often "every man did that which was right in his own eyes."

During these years of struggle some of the people of Israel fell into the Canaanitish customs and religion. The stern demands of the law and the covenant they had made with God gave way before the less demanding gods of the Canaanites called "Baals." But always God raised up a leader who was faithful and recalled the people to their God.

One of the best judges was Samuel. While he was yet a young boy, he helped Eli, the priest, at the house of worship. He was called of God to lead the people. He encouraged them against their enemies, helped them to know right from wrong, and reminded them over and over of God. "Hitherto the Lord has helped us," he reminded them. "He will help us now. Let us be his faithful people."

As Samuel grew old, the people of Israel said to him, "Let us have a king over us that we may be like all the nations, and so that our king may govern us and go out before us and fight our battles."

Samuel reminded them that a king also made heavy demands upon the people and counseled them to trust God only. But they wanted a king. So a handsome young man, tall and brave, was chosen to be king. His name was Saul, and Samuel anointed Saul king before all the people.

The Story of the Nations

The story the Bible tells shows how God continued to be with his people in spite of their repeated failures to remember the covenant they had made with God to be his faithful people.

It tells of the early struggles of the people under their king, Saul, of his victories, his sins, and his illness. It tells of the rise of David from being a shepherd boy to being a musician to the sick king, then becoming a famous soldier and popular hero, and close friend of Jonathan, the king's son. It tells how Saul became jealous of David, tried to kill him, and sent him into exile. It tells how David became the leader of a strong band of outlaw soldiers, how he saved the king's life when Saul was at his mercy. It tells of the death of Saul and Jonathan and of David's becoming king. It tells of David's strength and skill in establishing Israel as a strong nation with Jerusalem as its capital.

The story continues after the death of David with the reign of his son, Solomon. It tells of the splendor and greatness of Israel while Solomon was king, and of the building of the great Temple of God at Jerusalem. It tells, too, of Solomon's oppression of the people, and of the neglect of the covenant of God, even while the magnificent Temple was being built. Thus the seeds of the nation's downfall were sown during its period of greatest glory.

After Solomon's death there was revolt against the oppression that continued under his son. The kingdom was divided. The northern part of the country retained the name Israel, and the southern part was called Judah. Israel never again was great as a nation among the other nations of the earth.

In spite of their weakness, however, these two small nations were important in the history

King Jehu of Israel prostrating himself before the Assyrian king, Shalmaneser III.

The "Chronicle of Nebuchadnezzar," a stone engraving which dates the first fall of Jerusalem.

Assyrian warriors battling Arabs.

of mankind. For here was something unique.

Sometimes under good kings and more often under bad, and in spite of many failures and much suffering, there was always preserved a part of the people who listened to God and trusted him. And so the law of God and the worship of God were preserved among men.

But the nations themselves fell. First, Israel was conquered by Assyria, and then Judah was seized by Babylonia. The record in the Bible says that Israel and Judah fell to the mighty nations around them because the rulers and the people broke their promise to be God's people and to worship him only. Thus the history of these two nations tells the story of the righteousness of God, and of the suffering which comes to men and nations when they separate themselves from God.

The Great Prophets

During all the time Israel was a great nation and during the time when the two nations of Israel and Judah were in existence, there were in the land men who had more influence on history than did the kings. These men were called "prophets." They spoke for God. They stood against the kings when the kings did wrong, and they stood against popular opinion when the people refused to obey God. Often they were listened to with respect, and sometimes with fear. But often, too, they were scorned and arrested and persecuted when they preached what the king or the people did not want to hear.

Some of the prophets were traveling preachers who went about the country calling the people to turn from their evil ways and obey the commandments of their God. Elijah was one of these. He was distressed to see the people worshiping false gods, bringing gifts to the altars of the Baals and making prayers to them. The Bible tells a dramatic story of a challenge which Elijah issued to the prophets of Baal to meet him on Mt. Carmel for a test of strength between them, as each prayed to his God. The story is told in I Kings 18.

Elijah was fearless in speaking for God against kings and in keeping before the people during dark days the power of God to help them. Elijah's successor was Elisha, and he continued the vigorous proclamation of "thus saith the Lord."

But there were other prophets who were even more influential among the people of God during their own day and in the generations that followed. These were the prophets who not only preached but who also wrote down their messages.

The prophet Isaiah was an aristocrat who had access to the king's court, but he did not speak softly to the king. His boldness caused him to lose favor at court, so he used other means of speaking for God. He made signs to read and stood by the wayside where the king's chariot passed. And he preached to the people,

taught young men to be prophetic, and wrote many stirring words.

> Hear, O heavens, and give ear, O earth,
> For the Lord hath spoken:
>
> Some have I reared and brought up,
> But they have rebelled against me.
>
> ... Israel does not know,
> my people does not understand.

Jeremiah was another great writing prophet who suffered for his devotion to God's way when kings and people turned away. He was put in stocks where people gathered and jeered at him; he was put into a dungeon; his writings were destroyed. But he steadfastly called both kings and people to remember God and to obey him.

Amos was a countryman who came to the capital city and boldly went to the altar where the king worshiped. There he denounced both king and people for their oppression of the poor, their cheating in the market place, their injustices, their lives of extravagance and ease.

A reconstruction of Babylon, where the Israelites were captives. Tower of Babel in the foreground.

Hosea spoke more tenderly to his people. Because he himself had suffered betrayal by the wife whom he loved, he better understood the meaning of the steadfast love of God for his children who had betrayed his love. He spoke of God's continuing love which would not let his people go but sought them always, even when they sinned.

All the great prophets who lived in Israel and Judah pled with the people to keep the covenant to be God's people, to trust God. They warned against putting trust in armies or in other nations. They proclaimed to kings and people alike that to turn against God was to bring suffering and disaster upon themselves and their children. Because God is righteous, they said, the nations would be punished for their sins. They would suffer. But the great prophets proclaimed also the love of God. Because God is God and not man, they said, God's love for his people will not cease because they turn against him. He will win them back.

In Captivity

After Israel and Judah were overthrown, most of the people were taken away by the conquerors to work for the rulers of their lands. The descendants of the patriarchs, whom God had once brought out of slavery in Egypt and led to nationhood, now were captives again. Because they had forsaken God, they became aliens in strange lands, far from the home of their fathers, from Jerusalem, and from the Temple, the center of their worship.

After the people were taken into capitivity, the prophets were their comfort and their hope. For these great men of God kept alive the faith that God was still their God and would not forsake them.

Because some of the people believed what the prophets said, they continued to worship God and trust him even after their nations fell and they lived in foreign captivity.

Ezekiel, a great prophet of the period of

captivity, preached to the people continually that God is in control of the affairs of men and of nations, no matter how dark the times might seem to us.

In magnificent poetry and prose preserved in the latter part of the book of Isaiah, a great prophet proclaims the might of God and his continuing help to his people:

Have you not known? Have you not heard?
The Lord is the everlasting God, the
  Creator of the ends of the earth.
He does not faint or grow weary, his
  understanding is unsearchable.
He gives power to the faint, and to
  him who has no might he increases
  strength. . . .
They who wait for the Lord shall renew
  their strength, they shall mount up
  with wings like eagles, they shall run
  and not be weary, they shall walk and
  not faint.

(Is.40:28–31)

And so the people in exile from their homeland continued to have faith that God would one day bring them again to the land of their fathers, that they would again worship in the Temple at Jerusalem.

The Bible record includes stories of heroes set in the time of the captivity which show how the people lived and suffered. Daniel is the one best known. He was a Hebrew, an exile, living in Babylon at the time of its greatness when Nebuchadnezzar was the powerful king. Through steadfastness to his God in spite of orders to worship images and consequent persecution, Daniel gave his people an example of strength and of devotion to God which inspired them to like devotion.

The story of Esther tells of a young woman of the people of Israel in Persia, another land of exile. Esther was chosen to be queen by Ahasuerus, the king. Through her act of courage at the risk of her own life, she was able to defend her people against schemes of their enemies to destroy them.

In the Bible there are also poems which tell of the grief of the people in captivity, and of their longing to return to their homeland. They interpret, too, the meaning of their suffering and grief. There are dirges over the destruction of Jerusalem.

How lonely sits the city
    that was full of people!
How like a widow has she become,
    she that was great among the nations!
She that was a princess among the cities
    had become a vassal.
She weeps bitterly in the night.

The roads to Zion mourn,
    for none come to the appointed feasts.
All her gates are desolate,
    and she herself suffers bitterly.

The Lord has made her suffer
    for the multitudes of her transgressions;
All her people groan
    as they search for bread.
"Look, O Lord, and behold,
    for I am despised."

(LAM. 1:1, 2, 4, 11)

But in this poetry from the captivity there is also faith in God's continuing love for his people.

The steadfast love of God never ceases,
    his mercies never come to an end;
They are new every morning;
    great is thy faithfulness.
The Lord is good to those who wait for him,
    to the soul that seeks him.

(LAM. 3:22, 23, 25)

The Return from Captivity

The Bible story says that there came a time when in the providence of God the people of Israel—or the Jews, as they came to be called during the captivity—did return from the foreign lands to which they had been taken. They did return to the land of their fathers, but what they saw as they returned caused them deep grief. Their beloved city of Jerusalem was in ruins, her walls destroyed, her great Temple but rubble.

Now, Nehemiah was a Jew who had become cupbearer to the king of Persia at his palace,

and had won the favor of the king. When Nehemiah heard about the condition in which Jerusalem had been found, he was deeply distressed. He prayed to God for courage. Then he dared approach the king and ask to be allowed to go to Jerusalem and help rebuild the city. The Persian king granted Nehemiah's request. He also was moved to provide help for the rebuilding.

Nehemiah inspired fresh courage in the discouraged people who had returned. He spurred them to heroic action in spite of the taunts of enemies and efforts to discredit him and to divert him from his work. And so the wall was built again around Jerusalem.

The Temple for the worship of God was also rebuilt. And Ezra, the scribe, gathered the people together to teach them the Law of God which some of them had forgotten.

Not all the Jews returned to the land of their fathers. Many of those who had been taken into captivity had grown old. Many others who had been taken captive when they were little children and had grown up in the foreign country, continued to live there.

Those who did come back came to be called the "remnant," or the remaining small part of the people of Israel. It is with this remnant back in Jerusalem that the Old Testament story ends.

But the returning Jews were not an independent nation. First they were ruled from Persia, then from Greece, then Syria. Often they were discouraged. They sometimes asked God, "How hast thou loved us?" and "Where is the God of justice?" But through all their suffering they held fast to their faith that God was with them and would send a deliverer.

The last chapter of the Old Testament repeats the call of God to his people: "Remember

the law of my servant Moses that I commanded him for all Israel," and the promise of God to be with his faithful people. "For you who fear my name the sun of righteousness shall rise with healing in its wings" (MALACHI 4:2).

In the writings which tell what happened between the time of the Old Testament and the time of the New Testament—some books in the collection called the Apocrypha—there is the account of a terrible persecution of the Jews by Antiochus Epiphanes. The Temple was desecrated by bringing into the sacred place the trappings of the worship of heathen gods. This caused a fiery revolt under Judas Maccabeus which ended victoriously. For about a hundred years the Jews were again independent. It was to them a glorious time.

But the little country stood in the way of powerful nations struggling to control the world. And the faithfulness of the Jews to their own unique religion stirred up suspicion and hatred among other peoples. When Rome became the great world power, her armies conquered the land, and once again the Jews became a subject people. They had a ruler appointed by Rome. Yet into this conquered nation God came in a new and glorious way. Here Jesus Christ was born.

Chart I. THE BIBLE STORY AS IT HAPPENED

Scholars have long been searching ancient manuscripts and monuments and sites of time-buried cities to help them place the events recorded in the Bible each at the correct time in human history. It began so long ago! They do not know the exact date of each event recorded. It is especially hard to find the date of the earliest events. This is the time line which most of the scholars think is approximately correct. The chief persons who lived during each period are named under the event.

ABOUT WHEN IT HAPPENED	EVENTS AND PERSONS
In the beginning	*Creation* (Before human history began)
As the generations passed	*The Great Flood* : NOAH and his SONS
About 2000 to 1400 B.C.	*The Patriarchs* : ABRAHAM, ISAAC, JACOB, (later called Israel), JOSEPH / *Sojourn in Egypt* / *Birth of Moses*
About 1250 B.C.	*Exodus from Egypt*
About 1200 B.C.	*Conquest of Palestine by Hebrews* : JOSHUA, GIDEON, SAMSON, SAMUEL
About 1000 B.C.	*The United Kingdom of Israel* : SAUL, DAVID, SOLOMON (Temple built about 930 B.C.) Division of the kingdom (about 933 B.C.)
About 900 B.C.	*Israel* (Northern part of united kingdom) : ELIJAH, ELISHA / *Judah* (Southern part of united kingdom)
About 800 B.C.	*The Great Writing Prophets* : AMOS, HOSEA, ISAIAH, MICAH / *The fall of the northern kingdom (Israel)* 721 B.C.
About 700 B.C.	*Finding the Book of Law* (621 B.C.) : JEREMIAH
About 600 B.C.	*Fall of Jerusalem* (586 B.C.) : EZEKIEL / *Period of Exile* (586–538 B.C.) / *Return to Jerusalem* (538 B.C.) / *Temple rebuilt*
About 500 B.C.	*Nehemiah rebuilds the wall of Jerusalem* / *Ezra teaches the Law to the people*
About 400 B.C.–300 B.C.	*Palestine under foreign rulers—Persian, Greek*
About 200 B.C.	*Maccabean revolt and victory* (165 B.C.)
About 100 B.C.	*Roman conquest of Palestine* (63 B.C.)

THE BIRTH OF JESUS

First century A.D.	*The ministry of Jesus* / *The work of the disciples with Jesus* / *The crucifixion of Jesus* (about 30 A.D.) / *Paul's conversion* (about 35 A.D.) / *Beginning of Christian church* / *Dispersal of the Apostles* (about 44 A.D.) / *Spread of Christianity to gentile world* / *Persecution of the Christians under Nero and Domitian* (64–96 A.D.)
On to the Future	*Prophesy of the Triumph of God* (*Revelation*)

The Story the New Testament Tells

AS the Old Testament tells, the people of Israel were God's people in a special sense. God had chosen them to hear his word and to make it known to all men. God had made a covenant with them. God had revealed to them his power, his steadfast love, and his righteousness through his acts in creation, through the prophets, and through the events of their own history. But they had been slow to learn. They had not responded to God, and so they had suffered national defeat and religious persecution. Yet always there was a faithful remnant among the people who kept alive the covenant with God and the faith that he would redeem his people.

When they were discouraged about the present, there was the expectation in their faith that God would one day raise up a great leader who would save them. Often their expectations seemed to be for the coming of a great heavenly warrior who would overthrow all their enemies and restore the greatness of the nation as it had been under King David. In this coming age there would be peace among the nations, with Jerusalem the capital of the world.

But some of the great prophets spoke of the coming of the Kingdom of God in different terms. The people of Israel were God's chosen people, they taught, but not because God loved them more than other peoples and intended for them to triumph over other nations. Rather, God had chosen them to help other peoples know God. They were called, not to be the mightiest nation on earth, but rather to be a people who were willing to suffer for the sake of others. They were called to be a people who were willing to take the part of servants working to help others, rather than that of rulers controlling other peoples.

These ideas were not pleasing to many of the people. They found it hard to give up their dreams of national greatness and power for themselves.

But in the course of time the ideas of the greatest prophets proved to be right. For the One who came to live among men was not a warrior nor a king nor one who reestablished a great nation. The One came as a helpless baby, grew up as a child in the home of a village carpenter, never had a house to call his own, and spent his life helping all who needed him and showing them God's love.

The New Testament sets forth God's new covenant with his people in Jesus Christ.

When Jesus Came Among Men

The first four books in the New Testament tell about the life and teachings, the death and resurrection of Jesus. The account begins with the birth of a baby in a stable on a night of wonder. It tells of shepherds who saw glorious light and heard a heavenly chorus. It tells of the visit of Wise Men from afar. It tells very briefly of the boy's growing up and then of his ministry of love.

The New Testament tells how Jesus helped people, by teaching them what God is like and what he calls man to be.

Jesus Showed Men God's Love

Most important, Jesus helped people by *showing* them as he lived among them. By his concern for the friendless and the sick, he showed the people that God cared for them. By his thoughtfulness for children, he showed men the tenderness of God. By his willingness to be friends with and to help people of other nationalities and races, he showed them that God loves all men. By his condemnation of greed and hatred and false pride, he showed them the righteous judgment of God upon evil. By his forgiveness of those who sinned, he showed men God's mercy. By his joyousness amid simple things, he showed men that when they live close to God, many *things* are not important to happiness. He showed them that loving God and loving others are what make for happy, abundant living.

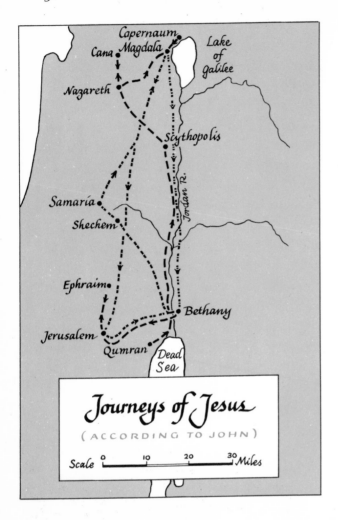

Journeys of Jesus
(ACCORDING TO JOHN)

Scale 0   10   20   30 Miles

Jesus traveled by foot all about his country, teaching in synagogues, on the side of a mountain, by the lake shore—anywhere there were people to listen. As he traveled, he stopped along the roadside when he saw some who needed help: a blind man, a sick child, a man who had no friends, a woman who had done wrong and was in danger of being stoned by a self-righteous mob.

He chose twelve men to be his special friends and helpers. These men were called disciples. They were not men the world considered important—several were fishermen, one was a tax collector, another probably an ex-soldier—but they loved Jesus and traveled with him and went to other places for him. Very little is told about most of the disciples. Peter, James, and John seem to have been the ones whom the others accepted as leaders.

Jesus taught that being close to God is what makes life happy and secure and good, and that turning away from God is what makes life sad and fearful and miserable. Sometimes he told stories, called parables, to make this meaning

The Disciples of Jesus

The special disciples of Jesus called apostles were these:

SIMON, *whom Jesus called Peter; and* ANDREW, *his brother. They were fishermen.*
JAMES *and* JOHN, *the sons of Zebedee, who also were fishermen.*
PHILIP, *who asked Jesus, "Show us the Father."*
BARTHOLOMEW, *about whom the Bible tells us nothing more.*
THOMAS, *whose doubts about Jesus were set to rest.*
MATTHEW, *who was a despised publican or tax collector for the Romans.*
JAMES, *the son of Alphaeus, about whom nothing more is told us.*
THADDAEUS, *about whom the Bible tells nothing more.*
SIMON, *who was called the Zealot, or strong nationalist.*
JUDAS ISCARIOT, *who betrayed Jesus.*

MATTHEW 10:2-3

clear. He told one story about two men who built houses. One of them built on a good rock foundation. The other built on sand. Both the houses looked pleasant while the weather was calm. But when the storms beat upon each house, the house that was built on sand fell, and the house that was built on the solid rock foundation was secure. So will those be who trust God.

To make clear that God forgives his children and restores them to their place in his family, he told a story about a son who wanted to leave home and go his own way. His father gave him a part of the family money, and the boy went to a far country where he wasted his inheritance in wicked living. He came to himself and was sorry. He decided to return to his father's house and ask for forgiveness. As he drew near, his father ran forward to meet him and rejoiced over his return.

Because Jesus spoke so simply, and because in his life he *showed* people God's love and concern for them, the people heard him gladly. Great crowds came and listened eagerly. "No man ever spoke as this man" is the way one man reported. Thus he enabled men to be hopeful and thankful rather than anxious and fearful.

Those Who Opposed Jesus

But there were others, many of them important people in the land, who opposed Jesus. There were "parties" in Jesus' time, as in our own. They were not much like political parties as we know them, but they divided the people.

The Pharisees were leaders of the Jewish people who were very zealous for the old Jewish law. They thought Jesus was wrong in being friends with tax collectors and sinners who did not keep the ceremonial law. They thought he was wrong in teaching people that being loving and kind and keeping close to God through prayer were more important than observing all the customs and rituals in the religion of their fathers, and more important than money and position. They thought Jesus was criticizing their faith when he put loving

The Sea of Galilee with Mt. Hermon (the Mount of the Transfiguration) in the background.

God and loving others above the forms and rules of their worship. They thought he was destroying their influence among the people. So they turned against him.

The Sadducees were the important and often wealthy people who frequently were appointed to important positions in the Temple because they were in favor with the Roman conquerers. They were against Jesus because he threatened their privileges.

The Zealots were the fiery patriots, the "nationalists," who wanted to raise armies and fight the Romans to regain independence for the Jews. They decided Jesus was not the warrior leader they needed, and so they turned against him.

The Crucifixion of Jesus

Among all these influential people of his day Jesus lived. He disturbed them by what he was and by what he did. Their anger grew and so their opposition grew. They wanted to get rid of him. They made false charges against him.

Finally, Jesus was brought before the Roman court and charged with stirring up the people against Caesar, the head of the great Roman Empire which had conquered their land.

Pontius Pilate was the governor of Judea appointed by Rome. Pilate did not want to condemn Jesus, but he was afraid to ignore the charge that Jesus was stirring up trouble against the Roman State lest he offend the emperor and the important people in the land he governed. So he gave the word and turned Jesus over to the Roman soldiers.

The disciples were not with him now. When Jesus was arrested, they had fled in the darkness. When Peter was questioned, he denied he even knew him. In fear, the disciples had hid in a secret place. So Jesus was alone. The soldiers led him away to be put to death by the cruelest form of execution, crucifixion.

A part of the Garden of Gethsemane, with olive trees centuries old.

Though the soldiers and some of the crowd jeered at him, as Jesus hung in agony he prayed for them: "Father, forgive them, for they know not what they do." And so he died.

The Power of God's Love

But the story of Jesus does not end here. What happened next made all the difference. The frightened friends of Jesus had a wonderful experience. Jesus made himself known to them. They knew that Jesus was with them again. He was alive! They were not alone! They would never be alone again.

God had proved that he was mightier in his power and purpose than the rulers of the great Roman Empire. He could change their verdict. They had decreed that Jesus' life and influence should end. God's purpose was that Jesus should continue to be in the lives of men. God's love was stronger than the power of men to kill and the hatred of men that made sin in the world. Jesus, whom sinful man had put to death, by the power of God lived again. God's holy spirit would be with his children forever.

The story in the New Testament tells how the disciples lost their fear. They became new men, made over by their faith in the living Christ. And by their witness they changed the history of the world.

The Disciples Tell the Good News

The New Testament continues the story. It tells the story of how the friends of Jesus changed. The frightened men, hiding in an upstairs room after the crucifixion for fear that they too might be arrested, became courageous preachers. The New Testament tells how they proclaimed that God had sent Jesus to men, that sinful men had

Ruins of the Temple of Apollo in Corinth. Paul must have seen this temple on his journeys.

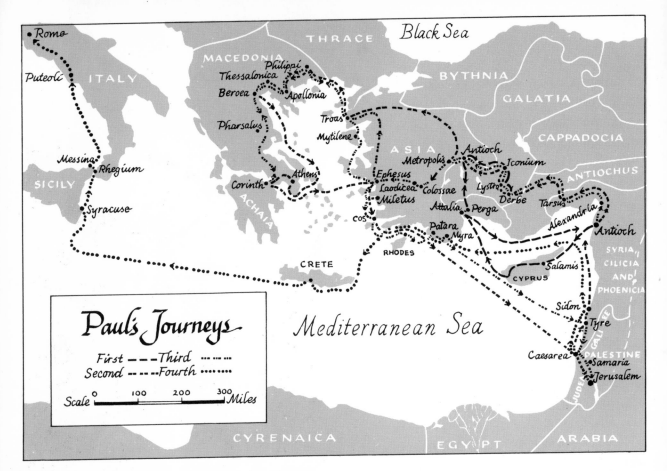

Paul's Journeys

First --- Third ....
Second ----- Fourth ....

Scale 0 100 200 300 Miles

caused Jesus to suffer and die, but that God had triumphed over their evil plans, and that Jesus had conquered death.

This courageous proclamation attracted wide attention. Great crowds gathered to listen, and thousands were convinced that what the disciples were saying was true. More and more people became followers of Jesus.

Now the disciples were in conflict with the leaders of the country. They were arrested and taken to court. But they spoke boldly, telling without fear what they knew was true.

The faith spread "in Jerusalem, in Judea, in Samaria, and unto the uttermost parts of the earth." And this in spite of opposition of the rulers, persecution, and even misunderstandings among the followers of Jesus themselves.

Peter and John and James were the leaders of the followers of Jesus who were in the home country, Jerusalem and Judea.

Paul Tells the Good News

Paul was a remarkable world traveler and preacher. He began by persecuting the followers of Jesus. He took part in the stoning to death of Stephen, the first Christian martyr. Then he had a wonderful experience. He came to know that what the disciples preached was true. He became a most courageous missionary to the Gentile world. In spite of persecution both by Jews and Gentiles, he sought to break down the barriers between them, calling them all to be devoted followers of Jesus. In one city where he preached, Antioch, the followers of Jesus were first called Christians.

Through years of devotion and hardships, brilliant preaching and writing, Paul made Christianity a world religion. He took it beyond Palestine, into Asia Minor, to Europe, and all the way to the household of Caesar in Rome, the very center of the mighty empire.

The story the New Testament tells is carried forward through some of the letters which Paul wrote to the churches he had established.

The Christians in these churches to which Paul wrote had either been reared as Jews, as Paul and all the disciples had been, or they had been reared in a pagan religion. They had heard Paul tell them about how God had made himself known through Jesus Christ who had lived among men. They had heard Paul tell the good news that God loved men and had saved them from their sin and made possible for them a new and good life. They had listened to this good news. They wanted this new life for themselves.

These early Christians lived in cities where they were a tiny minority. Most of the people and all the rulers ridiculed them and made all sorts of trouble for them. They needed help in understanding their new faith, and encouragement in standing fast for it in spite of abuse by the people about them. They needed to have

The Emperor Nero, who persecuted the Christians.

explained to them just what God's purposes for them as shown in Jesus Christ called upon them to be and to do in everyday living.

And so Paul wrote letters telling them more about Jesus and what he did for men. With this help, the young churches survived in spite of great difficulties. Paul assured the members of the churches that the church would survive because it was of God. And so it has.

Being a Christian in the First Century meant more than just belonging to a church and professing a creed. It was often literally a matter of life and death. It seems clear that Peter and James and Paul were all put to death for their faith in Jesus Christ.

Under the Roman emperors, Nero and Domitian, persecution was especially fierce and

cruel. Emperor worship was established, and with this the Christians could not compromise. They could worship God only.

Toward the Future Triumph of God

The last book in the Bible, the book of Revelation, reflects these desperate times for the Christians. It is written in symbolic language so that the officials seeking out Christians for arrest would not understand it. But the message had meaning for those who received it. In vivid pictorial language, it showed to the hard-pressed Christians the great eternal power of God arrayed against the cruelty of the oppressor. And it shows that God triumphs!

Revelation is a book about the future. After terrible convulsions, the new heaven and the new earth will emerge, and amid its beauty the faithful servants of God will dwell with him in glory. God "will wipe away every tear from their eyes, and death shall be no more, neither shall there be mourning nor crying nor pain any more" (REV. 21:4).

So the story the Bible tells ends with the triumph of God in conquering evil and sin and winning his children to respond to his love. "The kingdoms of this world have become the kingdoms of our Lord and of his Christ, and he shall reign forever and ever" (REV. 11:15).

The Triumph of God

Behold the dwelling of God is with men. He shall dwell with them, and they shall be his people, and God himself will be with them; he will wipe every tear from their eyes, and death shall be no more, neither shall there be mourning nor crying nor pain any more.

And the city has no need of sun or moon to shine upon it, for the glory of God is its light. By its light shall the nations walk; and the kings of the earth shall bring glory into it.

The kingdoms of this world are become the kingdoms of our Lord, and of his Christ; and he shall reign forever and forever.

REVELATION 21:3-4; 11:15 (KJV)

How Did the Bible Come to Be?

NOW that we have reviewed the story the Bible tells, let us see how this story came to be told.

We are so accustomed to seeing copies of the Bible, nicely printed and bound into books, that the Bible is taken for granted as a book which it is easy to get, to read, to use. So it is in the United States today. But it came to its present form through thousands of years and the work —and sometimes the death—of many devoted persons who were sure they were called of God to make his word known. It has required much suffering and struggle to give man the Bible.

In the beginning, the Bible did not look at all like the copies in our homes and churches and libraries today. How did the Bible begin?

The Bible itself says it began with God. God, who called men to love him and trust him and obey him, chose many ways to help man understand his purposes. One way was through thoughtful and gifted persons who were especially responsive to God. Because these persons were especially able to understand what God was making known to his children, they could help other persons know God. God chose such men to work with him. They were real men who lived in a real place and at a real time in history. They lived in the part of the world we call the Holy Land. They were Hebrews, who came to be called the people of Israel. But they were not ordinary men. Today we say they were inspired by God.

First through spoken words, these persons in the long ago told the others what they had come to understand of the greatness and goodness of God. These words were listened to because they seemed good and wise. The words were memorized. They were taught by fathers to children and from one family to another. By and by, as men learned to write, they were written down.

We do not know just what were the very first words of the Bible that were written down, nor exactly when nor where nor by whom the first ancient words were written. It all happened long, long ago.

The Beginnings of the Scripture

The people of Israel had a long history and many writings before there were libraries for keeping writings together.

So far as we know, the first actual book to be taken care of as sacred writings or Scripture by the people of Old Testament times was a book found in the Temple at Jerusalem.

There had been a period in the history of Israel when the people had neglected the worship of God. The words of the prophets and the religious writings of earlier times were ignored. The kings did "that which was evil in the sight of the Lord," and the people forgot what their fathers had taught them about God and his purposes. The Temple had fallen into disrepair.

Then a new king came to the throne, King Josiah. He wanted to restore the worship of God. He set workmen to cleaning and repairing the Temple. As this work was going on, a large scroll, or book, was found. The scroll was taken to the king and read to him. As he heard it, the king realized that this was the book of the law of God. It had been lost in the unused Temple. Now the book of God had been found! The king ordered the book read to the people. What was written in the book the king proclaimed to be the law of the land, because it was God's law. The dramatic story of the finding of this book is told in II Kings: 22–23.

This scroll contained what is in our Bibles now as the book of Deuteronomy. It includes some rituals and ceremonies. Much more important in this book is the strong setting forth of God's call to be his people and to live righteously in the nation and in relationships among persons. It calls for the remembrance of God in all the affairs of life.

Chart II. HOW THE BIBLE CAME TO BE

Old Testament

DATE	WHAT WAS DONE TO GIVE MEN THE BIBLE
In the Beginning	*God's purpose to make himself known / Men who were responsive to God / Early poems, laws, accounts of events / Records on stones and monuments*
About 1200 B.C.	*Early writings / Accumulation of laws, poems, biographies*
800 B.C.	*The Writing Prophets*
621 B.C.	*Finding the Book of the Law in Temple*
400 B.C.	*Bringing together of the Law (Pentateuch)*
200 B.C.	*Bringing together of History and Prophets (the Law and the Prophets)*
100 B.C.	*Bringing together of the Writings*
90 A.D.	*Closing of Old Testament Canon*

New Testament

DATE	WHAT WAS DONE TO GIVE MEN THE BIBLE
To A.D. 30	*The life of Jesus / The ministry of the Apostles*
Middle of first century A.D.	*Paul's preaching and writing / Epistles (letters of Paul)*
Latter half of first century A.D.	*Writing of Gospels and Acts / Other Letters (dates of some not clear) / Revelation*
Second and third century A.D.	*The Church uses the Christian writings along with Old Testament Scripture*
Middle of third century A.D.	*Closing the New Testament Canon*

Some Ancient Sacred Books Not Included in the Canon of the Scriptures

BOOKS IN THE APOCRYPHA

ESDRAS

TOBIT

JUDITH

ESTHER (*additions to the book in the Old Testament*)

WISDOM OF SOLOMON

ECCLESIASTICUS

BARUCH

SONG OF THE THREE CHILDREN

BEL AND THE DRAGON

I AND II MACCABEES

With this scroll the people of Israel had the beginning of their permanent, written sacred library, their Scripture, which we today call the Old Testament.

The Record of God's Action in History

There were also in the land other writings, some of them very old. There were accounts of God's acts in creation and in calling great men and in saving his people. There were poems and codes of God's laws. There were stories of great men who loved and trusted God. These materials, too, were brought together and interpreted by faithful scribes, responsive to God. Slowly the Scriptures were taking form as a library of sacred writings.

These writings, the first to be called Scripture, are preserved in our Bible in the first five books of our Old Testament: Genesis, Exodus, Leviticus, Numbers, Deuteronomy. These books were referred to as The Law. For a long time these were the only books called Scripture.

But there were yet other writings in the land. There is mention in the Bible of some of these old writings which have not survived. There was a book called "The Book of Jashar," referred to in Joshua 10:13, and a poem from this writing is quoted in II Samuel 1:17–27. There is reference to and a quotation from a writing called "The Book of the Wars of the Lord" in Numbers 21:14–15. In I Kings 14:19 and 29 two other old books are mentioned, "The Chronicles of the Kings of Israel" and "The Chronicles of the Kings of Judah."

Devout men, responsive to God, were eager to bring all these records together and write an account of the acts of God in behalf of his people throughout the history of their nation.

The Books of the Law

GENESIS: *The creation; the first man; how sin began; the flood; stories of the great patriarchs and the people of Israel; Noah, Abraham, Isaac, Jacob, Joseph.*

EXODUS: *Story of Moses; the journey of the people of Israel from Egypt to Canaan; the giving of the Law at Mt. Sinai; the Ten Commandments; the covenant between God and his people.*

LEVITICUS: *The details of the ceremonies of worship and sacrifice and the duties of the priests.*

NUMBERS: *The journeyings of the children of Israel in the desert; the census of the people taken at Mt. Sinai, tribe by tribe.*

DEUTERONOMY: *The exposition of the faith of Israel in God who chose them and preserved them in spite of their disobedience; call to the people to love and serve the God of love and righteousness; account of the death of Moses.*

The Former Prophets (Books of History)

JOSHUA: *The entrance of the people of Israel into Canaan under leadership of Joshua, Moses' successor.*

JUDGES: *The days of strife to possess the land; Gideon, Samson, Deborah.*

I and II SAMUEL: *The beginnings of the nation of Israel; Samuel, the last judge; Saul, the first king; David, the great hero king.*

I and II KINGS: *The history of Israel and Judah; the brilliant reign of Solomon, then oppression and revolt and the division of the kingdom; the story of the kings, the people, and the prophets; the sin of the kings and people; the fall of the nations; the captivity.*

The Later Prophets

ISAIAH: *A collection of great prophetic writings and accounts of events in the life of the prophet and of the nations.*

JEREMIAH: *Accounts of the life and works of Jeremiah; his writing his message; his warning of the coming fall of the nation.*

EZEKIEL: *The writings of a great prophet of the exile who assured the people that God was in control.*

THE TWELVE: *Hosea, Joel, Amos, Obadiah, Jonah, Micah, Nahum, Habakkuk, Zephaniah, Haggai, Zechariah, Malachi. Writings of prophets of righteousness, love, and the work of God in history.*

The history of the peoples was to them a record of the acts of God, of his love and his righteous judgment.

This record came to be called the Former Prophets. It is preserved in our Bible as the books we think of as history: Joshua, Judges, I and II Samuel, I and II Kings.

The Writings of the Great Prophets

There were also being put into writing some materials that recorded the acts and sermons of the great prophets, the men who spoke for God to the kings and people alike.

There is kept for us in the Bible the story of how one of the great prophets, Jeremiah, wrote what God had called him to say to the people. He dictated it to a secretary called Baruch, who wrote it on a scroll. The words said that the king and the people would suffer because they had turned against the laws of God. When the words were read to the king, he was furious. He cut up the scroll with his pen knife and threw the fragments into the fire. Jeremiah's

There was also a rewriting of the history of the nation from the point of view of the priests, which came to be called I and II Chronicles. And there were accounts of the return from exile, now in our books of Ezra and Nehemiah.

These additional writings came to be used in public worship along with The Law and the Prophets. When the canon of the Old Testament was finally fixed in A.D. 90, these books were added as a third part. They were called the Writings.

These books are most varied, both in the form of writings and in content. I and II Chronicles and Ezra and Nehemiah have been mentioned in sketching the historical events. The other "writings" are primarily poetry, proverbs, and stories of the deeds of individual men and women of devotion and courage.

life was in danger for displeasing the king. But when he heard that the scroll had been burned, Jeremiah called Baruch and dictated it all over again. The story is told in Jeremiah 36.

The writings of the great prophets, when they were brought together, came to be called the Later Prophets.

After many years these records of the acts of God in the history of the people and the writings of the prophets came to be accepted as Scripture along with the books called The Law.

Now the Scriptures were called *The Law and the Prophets*.

Completing the Old Testament Scriptures

The devout Jews had also been developing devotional literature—poetry, hymns, and prayers for use in services of worship; proverbs and precepts about practical matters of everyday life; sermons; and stories of courageous persons who were true to their faith even in the midst of great danger.

The Writings

I and II CHRONICLES: *A second account of the history of Israel and Judah.*

EZRA and NEHEMIAH: *The return of a remnant of the children of Israel from captivity, the rebuilding of Jerusalem, the teaching of the law.*

ESTHER: *The story, set in a land of the exile, of a heroic young Jewish queen at the court of the king of Persia.*

JOB: *A great poetic work dealing with the question, "Why do good men suffer?"*

PSALMS: *The great hymns and poems of the faith of the people of Israel.*

PROVERBS: *A collection of practical wise sayings about everyday living*

SONG OF SOLOMON: *Poetry about human love.*

ECCLESIASTES: *Writings of an ancient preacher.*

LAMENTATIONS: *Poetry of sorrow over the fall of Jerusalem.*

DANIEL: *Story, set in Babylon, of a great Jewish hero who was faithful to God in a pagan society in spite of persecution, and the prophesy of the fall of the pagan nation.*

The most beloved and most frequently read is the book of Psalms. Most churches today read portions of the Psalms at each service. Psalm 23, the beautiful poem beginning "The Lord is my Shepherd," is one of the most familiar passages in the Bible.

Proverbs is a collection of wise sayings on many subjects, reflecting a down-to-earth way of dealing with everyday human problems and using everyday language. Here is one example:

Give me neither poverty nor riches;
feed me with the food that is
needful for me, lest I be full
and deny thee, and say, "Who is
the Lord?" or lest I be poor,
and steal, and profane the name
of my God.

(PROV. 30:8–9)

Job is a magnificent poetic work, dealing with the great question men have always asked,

"Why does God let good people suffer?"

The Song of Solomon is a collection of poems about human love.

Ecclesiastes, or "the preacher," presents rather a sad view of man's life, but includes some memorable passages, including the one beginning:

For everything there is a season,
And a time for every matter under heaven.

(Ecc. 3:1)

Lamentations consists of five chapters or poems lamenting the fall of Jerusalem, describing the suffering of the exiles, and offering prayer for God's mercy.

There are two books in the Bible named for women: Ruth and Esther.

Ruth is the story of the love of Ruth, the Moabite, for her mother-in-law, Naomi, a woman of Israel. It tells of the love of Naomi's kinsman, Boaz, for Ruth, which marriage founded the line from which King David came.

Esther is the story of the courage of the young Jewish wife of a powerful monarch in Persia who risked her life to save her people.

Daniel is a thrilling drama of the fearless faith of the Jews when they were subjected to persecution by foreign powers, and of God's deliverance. The latter part of the book is a prophesy of the downfall of the oppressors.

The Old Testament Canon

From the first written word to the closing of the Old Testament canon was a long time. But gradually the Old Testament books were completed and accepted as Scripture by the people of God: The Law, the Former Prophets (history), the Later Prophets, the Writings. The Old Testament canon was closed in 90 A.D.

From the time when the scholars think the first portions of the Old Testament were put into writing down to the time the canon was closed, more than a thousand years passed.

Beginnings of the New Testament

The writing of the New Testament was different. From the beginning there were written languages ready to be used. And the time that passed from the writing of the first portion of the New Testament until the last book was written was less than a hundred years.

The Letters to the Churches

No one knows for sure exactly what were the first written words now in our New Testament. But the earliest large portions of the New Testament to be written, as we now have them, were the letters written by Paul to the young Christian churches. These letters are called Epistles, which is the Greek word for letters. Most of the letters are given the name of the city to which they were sent.

PAUL'S LETTERS

To the Romans
First Letter to the Corinthians
Second Letter to the Corinthians
Letter to the Galatians
Letter to the Ephesians
Letter to the Philippians
Letter to the Colossians
First Letter to the Thessalonians
Second Letter to the Thessalonians
First Letter to Timothy
Second Letter to Timothy
Letter to Titus
Letter to Philemon

OTHER NEW TESTAMENT LETTERS

Letter to the Hebrews
Letter to James
First Letter of Peter
Second Letter of Peter
First Letter of John
Second Letter of John
Third Letter of John
Letter of Jude

These letters of Paul as they are now in our New Testament usually begin with a salutation to those to whom they were sent. For example, the letter to the Galatians begins:

> Paul an apostle . . . and all
> the brethren who are with me,
> To the churches of Galatia:
> Grace to you and peace from God
> the Father and our Lord Jesus
> Christ.
>
> (GAL. 1:1–3)

The letters often tell news of other Christians and send greetings from them. Sometimes the letter says that some friend wrote the letter for Paul or helped him write it.

For example, in the letter to the Romans there is a verse that tells us that a friend named Tertius wrote the letter as Paul dictated it: "I Tertius, the writer of this letter, greet you in the Lord" (ROMANS 16:22). In the first letter to the Corinthians, a verse says: "I, Paul, write this greeting with my own hand" (I CORINTHIANS 16:21). This seems to say that the rest of the letter was written by someone to whom Paul dictated it, but that Paul added a greeting in his own handwriting. And in the letter to the Galatians is this verse: "See with what large letters I am writing to you with my own hand,"

(Galations 6:11). This seems to suggest that Paul had trouble writing, perhaps because his eyes were bad, and so had to depend upon others to help him.

In the book called Ephesians the salutation says it is to "the faithful" rather than to any one church.

There are also some letters in the New Testament which are addressed to individuals rather than to churches, such as I and II Timothy, Titus, and Philemon. The book of Hebrews was probably written especially for the Jews who had become Christians, seeking to explain the significance of Jesus in terms Jews could understand.

The book of James is really a sermon rather than a letter. There are three books—I John, II John, and III John—which were letters written, they tell us, by "the elder" to the same group of Christians. Third John was addressed specifically to a man named Gaius, and I and II John to the church.

I and II Peter were not addressed to any specific person or church, and neither was the epistle of Jude. These letters were general epistles to the Christians.

The letters from Paul to the churches were precious to the churches to which they came. When Paul wrote the letters and when the churches first received them, it was not expected that they would become a part of the Scripture. They were letters from a respected leader to churches which needed counsel and help. These early Christians still regarded the Old Testament as Scripture. But the letters of Paul were so helpful that they were kept and read over and over again. After awhile the letters of Paul were shared, the church at one place sending the letter it had received to other churches and receiving letters in return.

Writing the Story of Jesus

In our New Testament today the first four books are Matthew, Mark, Luke, and John. These books tell about the birth, life, teachings, death and resurrection of Jesus. And so they are most loved. They are called the "Gospels." This is an old word which means "good news." It was good news to the world that Jesus had come to show men God's love.

The GOSPELS

MATTHEW

MARK

LUKE

JOHN

Some words of Jesus may have been written down while he was teaching. We do not know. But at first there was no need for a real written account of the life and teachings of Jesus. Jesus himself was with men. They could hear him first-hand as he taught them. They could see him first-hand as he helped people. There was no need to read about him.

It was all so different from anything they had heard or seen before. It meant so much to the people. They heard it gladly and remembered it.

After the crucifixion of Jesus, the disciples, those close friends of Jesus who had been with him most, went about the country preaching and teaching and helping people as they had seen Jesus do. These men had themselves lived close to Jesus and heard the words he said. They repeated them over and over. The people listened to the spoken word, and what they heard they told others.

But time passed. Some sayings of Jesus were written down. The disciples were scattered. Now the time had come when accounts of what Jesus had done and the words he had spoken must be brought together in writing.

Probably the first account of the life of Jesus to be put together in writing is within the book we now have in our New Testament as the Gospel of Mark.

Faithful followers of Jesus recalled what they had heard him say and what they had seen him do. Devout writers, called of God to preserve this record for the people of the world, wrote

Ruins of the synagogue in Capernaum, on the site where the disciples may have preached.

down what was remembered and what it had all meant to men. Luke tells how he wrote his account in Luke 1:1-4. And so the four Gospels were written, each one in its own way telling the same good news.

In both Matthew and Luke there is a good deal of material which is almost exactly like material in Mark. And both Matthew and Luke have some material not in any other gospel. For example, Matthew is the only one which tells the story of the Wise Men coming to visit the baby Jesus. (MATTHEW 2:1-12). And some parables, such as the one about the Wise and Foolish Virgins (MATTHEW 25:1-13), are found only in Matthew. Luke is the only one which tells the story of the shepherds and the angels (LUKE 2:8-20), and the beloved parables of the Good Samaritan (LUKE 10:25-37), and the Prodigal Son (LUKE 15:11-30).

John has more material that is different from all the others, and its point of view is more distinctive. It has the beautiful chapter which begins, "Let not your heart be troubled," and the great expression of Christian faith, "God so loved the world that he gave his only Son that whosoever believes in him shall not perish but have everlasting life."

But all four of the Gospels tell the same story of how God showed his redeeming love to man in Jesus Christ.

Mosaic floor of an ancient Christian church in Bethsaida, showing design of "loaves and fishes."

The New Testament as Scripture

As Christians moved out into the world, it was more and more important that they have a complete account of the life and teachings of Jesus. After the disciples and Paul had died, the written records became more and more necessary to the people. Now it became important that, in addition to the Old Testament Scriptures, there be Christian Scriptures. There was need for books which would be sacred for the Christians, telling them how the word of

››››››››››››››››Introduction to Luke's Gospel ‹‹‹‹‹‹‹‹‹‹‹‹‹‹

Inasmuch as many have undertaken to compile a narrative of the things which have been accomplished among us, just as they were delivered to us by those who from the beginning were eyewitnesses and ministers of the word, it seemed good to me also, having followed all things closely for some time past, to write an orderly account for you, most excellent Theophilus, that you may know the truth concerning the things of which you have been informed.

LUKE 1:1-4

God came to men through Jesus Christ.

There had come to be a number of Christian writings. The leaders of the Christian church selected the books which should be read in the churches as sacred books. They agreed first on the four Gospels: Matthew, Mark, Luke and John. Though put into writing by different men, these books were considered together as The Gospel.

The ACTS

The REVELATION

The Acts, which was a sort of second volume to the Gospel by Luke, was added as telling how the disciples carried on the work Jesus had left to them. As the churches read in these writings about the great work of Paul, they re-read with new appreciation the letters he had written to them. Now these letters were brought together from the various churches. The church leaders felt sure that God had in-spired Paul to write them. They too were accepted as Christian Scripture. Then other letters were added to be read in the churches. And finally the book of Revelation was added.

It did not take nearly so long for the New Testament books to be brought together as Scripture as it had taken for the Old Testament books. In 367 A.D. Athanasius, bishop of Alexandria, wrote down a list of Christian books accepted as scripture. These are the books we have in our New Testament today.

And so within the church, the New Testament canon was closed, and the Christian church had its own Scriptures, the New Testament, in addition to the Old Testament. The writing of the Bible was finished.

But few of the early Christian churches had copies of all the books of the Bible as we know them today. The writing of the books of the Bible was finished, but they were not easily available all together.

A papyrus roll (left) partially opened to show writing, and (right) closed, with seal and strings in place. Many portions of Biblical text were written on papyrus.

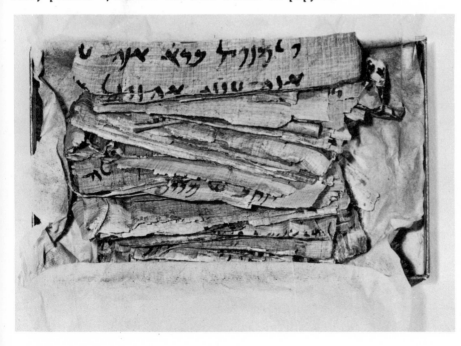

THE BIBLE is a Universal Portrait Gallery in which there are to be found pictures of all sorts of men and women. Kings and queens are here: Solomon importing for the amusement of his court ivory, apes and peacocks (I KINGS 10:22); the Queen of Sheba and her "very great retinue, with camels bearing spices, and very much gold, and precious stones" (I KINGS 10:2); Nebuchadnezzar demanding that all and sundry fall down and worship the great image of gold which he had set up, "whose height was sixty cubits and its breadth six cubits" (DANIEL 3:1).

Counselors to kings are here: Joseph, food administrator for the Egyptian government in a time of famine; Isaiah advising Ahaz not to be too greatly troubled at the presence of the Assyrian army, since (ISAIAH 7:14, 16) deliverance will be wrought; Nehemiah, cupbearer to Artaxerxes. Judges are here: Jephtha and Gideon and Samson. Reformers are here: Joshua destroying the high places of the Canaanites; Elijah wreaking havoc upon the priests of Baal; Josiah blotting out the worship of the false gods.

Great religious leaders are there: Abraham, venturing out not knowing where he was to go, but sure only that he could not go on living as he had been living; Samuel declaring that "to obey is better than sacrifice and to harken then the fat of rams" (I SAMUEL 15:22); Hosea who heard God say:

> "It was I who taught Ephraim to walk.
> I took them up in my arms; . . . . .
> I led them with cords of compassion,
> with the bands of love"   (HOSEA 11:4)

To these leaders God spoke, even though they were discouraged to the point of running away. To Moses the refugee "the angel of the Lord appeared . . . in a flame of fire out of the midst of a bush" (EXODUS 3:2). To the despondent Elijah God spoke in "the wilderness . . . under a broom tree" (I KINGS 19:4). To Jonah, rebelling against the divine compulsion to proclaim God's love to foreigners, God spoke in the shade of a castor oil plant (JONAH 4:6).

Bible History does not revolve about great names only. Common people are here, too, in great profusion: a village smithy filled with the Spirit of God (EXODUS 31:1-5); a peasant who defended the people with no weapon but an oxgoad (JUDGES 3:31); a smallholder who "had nothing but one little ewe lamb . . . and it was like a daughter to him" (II SAMUEL 12:3); loyal friends of David who risked their lives to get him

a drink from his favorite well (II SAMUEL 23:13-17); a land-owner who prized his patrimony so much he defied a king even though it cost him his life (I KINGS 21:1-14); fishermen who left their nets and tax-collectors who left the counting-house and carpenters who left the joiner's shop when the Lord of love came by; a devout man "looking for the consolation of Israel" (LUKE 2:25); a native of Cyprus whose comrades nicknamed him "Son of encouragement" (ACTS 4:36). These are they of whom it is written:

> *"they keep stable the fabric of the world,*
> *and their prayer is in the practice of their trade."*

No sacred book has so many worthy women: Hannah weaving a new robe each year and taking it to the boy whom she had lent to the Lord (I SAMUEL 1:27; 2:19); Naomi, who, though her lot was bitter, has given a new connotation to "mother-in-law"; a widow with a never failing cruse of oil; a homemaker who got her husband to add a special room to the house so they could take care of itinerant prophets (II KINGS 4:8-11); Rizpah, watching over the bodies of her slain sons "from the beginning of the harvest" until the rainy season began (II SAMUEL 21:10); a sinful woman who loved much because she was forgiven much (LUKE 7:36-50); Dorcas, whose death was mourned by poor people "showing coats and garments" which she had made and given away (ACTS 9:36-39); Eunice and Lois, who passed on a glorious heritage of faith to son and grandson (II TIMOTHY 1:5). In all the Gospels there is no instance of a woman who was hostile to Christ.

Children, too, are here: Joseph, a shepherd boy who was a dreamer of dreams; Samuel, a lad devoted to the service of the temple, who heard God speak at a time when "there was no frequent vision"; Isaiah, for whom a king's death was a shattering and transforming experience; Jeremiah, protesting when summoned to great responsibility: "Ah, Lord God! Behold, I do not know how to speak, for I am only a youth"; a servant girl who knew better than a general where help was to be obtained; a lad whose lunch, blessed by love, fed a multitude; a girl so filled with joy at hearing an apostle's voice that she rushed to tell others, leaving the door unopened. Small boys at Bethel made fun of a prophet's bald head. Children in Nazareth played at weddings and at funerals. Zechariah is sure that in the New Jerusalem "the streets of the city shall be full of boys and girls playing in its streets."

—*The Book God Made*, by J. Carter Swain. © 1959 by Hawthorne Books, Inc.

From Spoken Words to Printed Books

FROM the beginning of the Bible to the time when a first completed copy of all the books of both the Old Testament and the New Testament was carefully made by a devoted scribe was a long, long, long time. No one knows exactly how long. But the Bible itself says that God was in the beginning of the history of man on the earth, and that from the beginning God was seeking to make himself known to men. The Bible is the account of how God did make himself known.

Words, Stones, and Scrolls

As men who were responsive to God came increasingly to understand what God was showing them through his mighty acts in nature and in the affairs of man, they told others, and these told yet others. The words were memorized and faithfully repeated. Out of the telling there gradually came to be writings.

Perhaps these writings were first made on stones as reminders or monuments (see EXODUS 34:28, JOSHUA 24:27); then on the skins of animals; then on prepared scrolls (see JEREMIAH 36); then on papyrus rolls. As we have seen, there gradually came to be a body of sacred literature, a library called Scripture, made up of The Law, the Prophets, and the Writings. This was the Old Testament.

All these Old Testament books were written in the Hebrew language. They were written by hand on the scrolls or rolls. Early scrolls were made of animal skin, carefully chosen and treated. After the writing was done, the scrolls were rolled around rods for easier handling. Not all the scrolls were the same length—some of them were longer than others. Some of the Old Testament books were too long to be written on a single scroll, and so there would be more than one scroll or roll for a book. On other scrolls there might be included several shorter books. The longer rolls were heavy. In the writing there were no chapter or verse divisions as we have them in our Bibles now, so to read the scrolls required skill and understanding. Most of the people could not read them for themselves. The sacred writings were read aloud to the people.

Manuscripts

These writings on scrolls were called *manuscripts,* which means written by hand. Each word in our Bible was first written by hand on an ancient scroll.

The very first writings of the sacred words have all been lost. Even the first manuscripts of the whole Old Testament after it was brought together have been lost. How, then, do we know that the Bible we have today is "real"? How do we feel sure that the words we read are true to what was first written in the manuscripts by men inspired of God?

The story of how the manuscripts were copied, generation after generation, and with so few errors, is one of the wonderful stories of God's purpose and of man's faithfulness to God. Because they were sure that these sacred writings were in a unique sense God's way of making himself known to men, the men who copied the manuscripts did it with deep devotion and sense of responsibility.

Early copyists worked under the most careful supervision. We have some accounts of the rules laid down for the scribes, as the copyists were called. These rules were faithfully kept. The scribes were not allowed to write even a single letter from memory. Each one must be looked at in the text from which he was copying and copied one by one. Each line in the copy must be exactly counted, letter for letter, and compared to the manuscript from which the copy was being made. Thus it was made sure nothing had been added and nothing left out. All the time the scribe was work-

One of the Dead Sea Scrolls opened to a passage from Isaiah. Jesus may have read from such a scroll.

ing on the sacred text he must be in absolute silence. He could speak no words and no one could speak to him lest his attention be distracted from the copy.

When the nations of Israel and Judah fell and the people were taken into captivity away from their Temple and the land of their fathers, only their sacred writings, their Scriptures, were left to keep alive their religious faith. And so they were prized above all else. The Jews came to be known as the "People of the Book." Buildings called synagogues were erected where the people came regularly and here the Scriptures were diligently taught. More and more copies of the Scriptures had to be made.

During a period of terrible persecution, having the Scriptures was considered the mark of being a faithful Jew, and the conquerors wished to stamp out this religious faith. The Scriptures were ordered destroyed, and possession of a copy was a cause of death. So precious was their Scripture to them that many Jews suffered torture or death or exile to preserve their copies. But through the devotion of the faithful, copies of the Old Testament were saved.

As a result of this devotion and of the painstaking work of scribes, the text of the Hebrew Old Testament books was preserved, generation after generation.

In later years, a group of devoted scribes called the "Massoretes" were made responsible for standardizing the sacred text. After this, copies were made from this text. The oldest copy of the whole Old Testament in the Hebrew language now known to be in existence is in a Jewish synagogue in Syria. It is a copy of the Massoretic text.

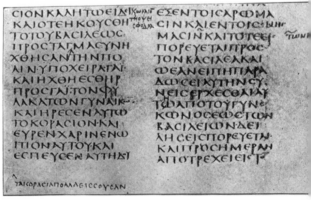

(Top) A portion of an early Greek version of the Bible (the Codex Sinaiticus), dating from the fourth century. Note that there is no punctuation or separation of words. (Left) a page from the Massoretic text of the Bible, written in Hebrew.

Translation of the Scripture Begins

Copying the Bible

Because of persecution, many Jews were scattered into other countries where Greek was the language of the people. So they learned to speak Greek. There was need for a translation of the Old Testament into Greek. A translation was made in the city of Alexandria by seventy-two scholars and so came to be called the "Septuagint." An old manuscript of this translation is now in the British Museum. Because the translation was made from a Hebrew text older than any Hebrew text now in existence, this Greek translation has been very important to the scholars in their effort to go back toward the exact wording on the first manuscript.

With the spread of Roman culture, the Latin language came into general use, and so translations were made into this language. The best known is the Vulgate, the work of the Roman scholar Jerome.

As was true of the Old Testament books, all the books of the New Testament in the handwriting of those who first put them into written form have been lost. But because the writings were very precious to the early Christians, the copies were made with the greatest care to avoid errors.

For years the only way the words of the Bible could be preserved was by these manuscripts or handwritten copies. This was true of both the Old Testament and the New Testament.

After the Christian church became established and grew and spread into many places, monasteries were established. Here were gathered devout men who gave their whole life to serving God through the church. The copying of the Bible was assigned to the monks in the monasteries. They became very skillful in this work. They learned to use material that could be folded into a book. And so the Bibles pro-

Chart III. SOME EARLY MANUSCRIPTS OF THE BIBLE NOW IN EXISTENCE

DATE	MANUSCRIPT
In the making for over 1000 years but no manuscripts of complete Old Testament now available which date earlier than 900 A.D.	**HEBREW OLD TESTAMENT** *The text was completed and fixed at Synod of Jamnia about 90 A.D. No early copies are in existence. Massorites standardized text about 250–300 A.D. The oldest copy of this text is from 900 A.D. The Dead Sea Scrolls provide Hebrew text of Isaiah and parts of other Old Testament in texts hundreds of years older. (Exact date of these manuscripts has not been fixed.)*
About 250 B.C.	**SEPTUAGINT** *(A Greek translation of the Old Testament made at Alexandria about 250 B.C. Only copies of this manuscript are in existence.)*
200–300 B. C.	**JOHN RYLANDS LIBRARY FRAGMENT** *Fragment of the earliest known copy of a Bible manuscript now in existence.*
170 B.C. to 68 A.D.	**DEAD SEA SCROLLS** *(Parts of Old Testament recently discovered.)*
384–405 A.D.	**VULGATE** *(Latin translation of Bible)*
About 350 A.D.	**CODEX VATICANUS** *(Vellum Bible in Greek)*
Early 4th century A.D.	**ALEXANDRINUS** *(Greek Bible)*
500–1500 A.D.	*Many illuminated manuscripts produced in monasteries, now in museums and libraries.*

duced in the monasteries looked more as our Bibles look today. But they were much, much larger and heavier!

There were special rooms in the monasteries set apart for the copying of the Bible, and special pens and special ink. There were also provided beautiful material upon which to write, and gold and colored paint with which to decorate the pages. Many of the Bibles which were produced in the monasteries were real works of art, richly decorated in glowing colors. Some old copies are today preserved in libraries and museums so people can see them. They are called "illuminated Bibles."

Suffering to Preserve the Bible

Just as the Jews suffered for their devotion to their Scriptures, Christians suffered for the Bible. There came times of new persecution for the church. In the days of the Emperor Diocletian, Christians suffered cruel torture at the hands of the Roman authorities for possessing portions of the Bible.

Even after Christianity became the accepted religion in the state, within the church itself there was persecution of those who sought to make the Bible available to the people. But a great new development was to help make the Bible known. With the invention of movable type during the fifteenth century, printing of the Bible became possible. Instead of having to be copied word for word by hand, one copy at a time, many copies could now be produced through one short operation. Now many more people could have the Bible. The invention of printing was a milestone in the story of the making of the Bible.

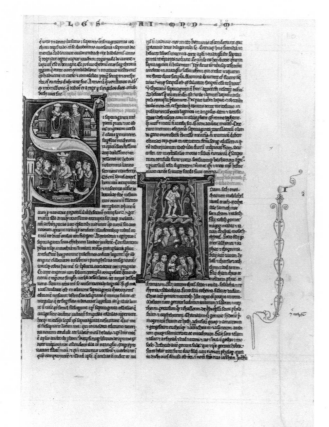

A page from a medieval illuminated Bible in Latin. The decorative initial letters were beautifully ornamented in gold and colors.

Into the Languages of the People

16 Oír is mar so do ghrádh-
uigh Día an domhan, go dtug

А Іоаннъ также крестилъ въ
потому что тамъ было ... воды ... , близъ Салима,
... приходили туда,

Ouine
trolar,
noctra

Aseken ne Niio tsini sakohnoronk8ahon

FOR many years after the writing of the Bible was completed, few people knew how to read. Only the leaders in the church could read. They would read the words of the Scriptures to the people and interpret them.

All the copies of the whole Bible were written in Greek or Latin, the languages used by scholars. But the people spoke other languages also. We call them today "modern languages" —German, French, English, and so on. The use of these languages grew. Fewer and fewer persons spoke the old languages. It became hard for the people to understand the Latin or Greek words of the Bible which were read to them.

Some church leaders thought the Bible should be translated into the language of the people. Others objected. They said the common people could not understand the Bible even if it were in their own language. It had to be interpreted to them by the leaders. A controversy arose, but the translators went ahead. Martin Luther made a translation into German, and other translations were made in other languages of the people. Many people learned to read just because they wanted so much to read the Bible.

As you read your Bible in English, you know that it is a translation from an ancient language in which the words were first written. But even the *English* translation has had a long history!

A laborer whose name was Caedmon is said to have produced the first bit of English literature by singing some paraphrases of the Bible in the Anglo-Saxon dialect. Bede, an early scholar who died in 735 A.D., translated the Gospel of John.

The oldest translation into English which is now available to men for study reads like this:

> Syle me, halig God,
> heortan claene.
>
> (PSALMS 51:10)

This is not the English people today understand. In present-day English the verse reads:

> Create in me a clean heart,
> O God.

58

Early English Translations

The first translation of the whole Bible into English was made by John Wycliffe over a hundred years before Columbus discovered America. In Wycliffe's translation the opening passage of Psalm 23 reads:

> The Lord gouerneth me and
> nothing in me shal lacke; in
> the place of leswe shall he me
> full sette.

About a hundred and fifty years later, William Tyndale made a new English translation of the New Testament. But now printing had been invented. Translation into the languages of the people and printing were important steps in making known the words of the Bible to the people. Several thousand copies of Tyndale's translation were printed. More and more people were learning to read, and they bought the copies eagerly.

The opposition of the church leaders to translation into the language of the people now in-

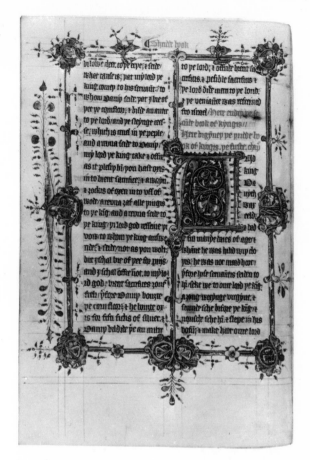

A page from Wycliffe's translation of the Bible into English. Note ornamentation of the text.

creased. Some leaders thought this widespread distribution of the Bible would lead to wrong understanding of the Bible. Some thought it would undermine the authority of the church to interpret the sacred word. Tyndale was put to death for printing and distributing the Bible in English. But nothing could stop the spread of the Bible among the people. They wanted to have it! So more and more work was done to make it available to the people. Gradually the opposition of the leaders lessened.

Through the years, as the English language changed in spelling and in the meanings of some words, scholars made new translations.

More English Translations

There came a time when it seemed good to get many of the best scholars together to make one English translation which would be as accurate as it could be made and which all the English-speaking people would use. The king of England, King James I, authorized the translation to be made. Forty-seven translators worked on it, beginning in 1604. They checked all the old manuscripts that could be found and sought to give the choicest meaning to every passage. This version was published in 1611. It became known as the "King James Version." For over three hundred years this was the version of the Bible most widely used in the English-speaking world. It continues to be beloved and cherished for its beautiful Elizabethan English. For example:

> The Lord is my shepherd, I shall
> not want. He maketh me to lie
> down in green pastures: he
> leadeth me beside the still
> water. He restoreth my soul.
>
> (PSALMS 23:1-3)

But the language of the people continued to change. This fact and other happenings called for new versions of the Bible. The archaeologists, men who study the ancient civilizations, were making exciting new findings of very old copies of the Bible. Materials long buried were found which threw light on the meaning of the ancient writings. Translators wanted to take advantage of this new knowledge to make the English translations more accurate.

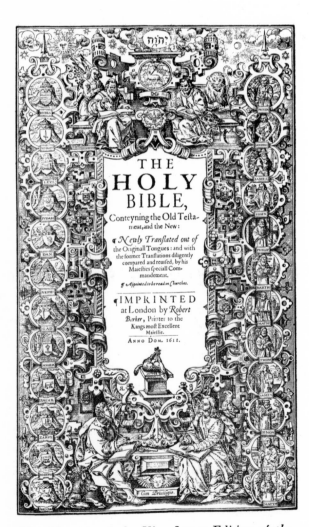

The title page of the King James Edition of the Bible, published in 1611.

Many Versions of the Same Text

Several translations and versions of the Bible in English were made during the three hundred years after the King James Version.

In 1952 there was published the Revised Standard Version of the Bible, the result of over twenty years of work by a large number of American scholars. It was accepted by most Protestant denominations of the United States as a clear, accurate rendering of the meaning of the ancient words. The English of the Revised Standard Version is simpler and more direct than that of the King James Version. Some mistranslations in the earlier versions are corrected.

Chart IV. SOME IMPORTANT TRANSLATIONS
OF THE BIBLE INTO ENGLISH

DATE	TRANSLATION
About 700 A.D.	*Caedmon's singing paraphrase of portions into Anglo-Saxon*
About 800 A.D.	*Bede's translation of Gospel of John*
871–901	*King Alfred's translations of portions*
Middle of tenth century	*Lindisfarne Gospel (A Latin translation, interlined with English)*
1380–84	*First translation into English of whole Bible under direction of Wycliffe*
1525–35	*Tyndale's translation of New and Old Testaments, the first English translation to be printed. It was completed by Coverdale.*
1582–1610	*Rheims' New Testament and Douai Old Testament published by Roman Catholic scholars. This was the standard text for Catholic Bibles for many years. It is known as the Douai Bible.*
1611	*King James Version of Bible. For more than 300 years the most widely used English Bible.*
1881–1885	*English Revised Version (New Testament, then Old Testament)*
1901	*American Standard Version*
1941–1951	*Confraternity New Testament and Old Testament (Catholic versions. New Testament, then Old Testament)*
1946–1952	*Revised Standard Version (New Testament, then Old Testament)*
1903–1960	*Several translations into modern forms of English—Moffatt, Goodspeed, J. B. Phillips and others.*

Scholars at work on the Revised Standard Version of the Bible, Old Testament section, in 1952.

Modern forms of words are substituted for the charming but sometimes misleading archaic terms of the King James Version.

For example, the King James Version says (PHILIPPIANS 4:14): "Notwithstanding ye have done well, that ye did communicate with my affliction." The Revised Standard Version translates it: "Yet it was kind of you to share my trouble."

There have also been some translations made into more informal, everyday sort of English to help people get the "feel" of the text. For example, in translating Romans 16:16, J. B. Phillips uses the form, "Give each other a hearty handshake all around for my sake," instead of using the literal translation, "Greet one another with a holy kiss."

Catholic Versions

The Roman Catholic Church has made translations of the Bible into English since 1582. The most widely used translation is the Douai Bible. This translation has been revised several times through the years.

In 1941 the Confraternity Edition began to be issued with official Catholic support, and this edition is generally accepted and used by American Catholics. It uses, for the most part, the modern forms of English words rather than the archaic forms.

Ronald Knox, an English Catholic scholar, published a new translation in 1944 which won acclaim from scholars and laymen alike.

In 1963 the Roman Catholic Church in England authorized a Catholic edition of the Revised Standard Version. So now Catholic and Protestant Christians have available a common version of the Bible.

Jewish Versions

Though many Jews have continued to teach their children the Hebrew language and continue to read the ancient language in some of their religious services, they have also made several translations of the Old Testament into English for general use in the synagogues and homes. The first such English translation was made in 1789. A new translation of the first five books of the Old Testament was published in 1959, and the other books are in process.

Variations in Translation

Not all the copies of the Bible in English today have exactly the same words in every verse. This is because there have been several translations into English. The scholars have sometimes used different English words to translate the same word in the ancient language.

Many translations of the Bible into English are available today. Some people think one translation is clearer, others think another translation is clearer. Everybody who reads the Bible in English today is reading a translation made by some devoted and careful scholar who loved the Bible and wanted to help people to understand what it says.

The Bible you read is probably called the King James Version or the Revised Standard Version or the Confraternity Edition. These are the translations which are most widely used in the United States today.

The Bible Around the World

There are, probably, in the world today more Bibles in the English language than in any other language. But there are also translations into many other languages. In some of them, like German and French and Spanish, there

A passage from John 3 translated into twelve languages. This is the famous passage beginning: "For God so loved the world that he gave his only begotten son, that whosoever believeth in him should not perish, but have everlasting life."

GREEK

Διότι τόσον ἠγάπησεν ὁ Θεὸς τὸν κόσμον, ὥστε ἔδωχε τὸν Υἱὸν αὑτοῦ τὸν μονογενῆ, διὰ νὰ μὴ ἀπολεσθῇ πᾶς ὁ πιστεύων εἰς αὑτόν, ἀλλὰ νὰ ἔχῃ ζωὴν αἰώνιον.

HEBREW

כִּי־אַהֲבָה רַבָּה אָהַב הָאֱלֹהִים אֶת־הָעוֹלָם עַד־אֲשֶׁר נָתַן אֶת־בְּנוֹ אֶת־יְחִידוֹ לְמַעַן אֲשֶׁר לֹא־יֹאבַד כָּל־הַמַּאֲמִין בּוֹ כִּי אִם־יִחְיֶה חַיֵּי עוֹלָם:

BULU

Amu beta nye'an, Zambe a nga nye'e bôte ya si nyô, a nga lôm atyi'i Mone dé, ajô te bôte bese môt a buni nye, a ye jañ, ve tabe ényiñ ya melu mese.

ESKIMO

Toiten Agaiutim tlamiut kinikkapigtshamíke kěngan Kitunrane tsikiutika, kina imna itlěnun ukfalra tamaskifkinako taugam nangiyuílingoramik unguvankriskluko.

NAVAHO

Háálá Diyin God nihokáá' dine'é t'áá'iiyisí 'ayóó-'áyó'níigo biYe' t'áálá'í bá yizhchíníigíí yeiníltį, 'áko t'áá háiida boodlą́ago ba'ólíhígíí 'éí doo 'ádoodjįł ďa, ndi 'iiná doo nínt'i'ii bee hólǫ́ǫ dooleel.

JAPANESE

神はそのひとり子を賜わったほどに、この世を愛して下さった。それは御子を信じる者がひとりも滅びないで、永遠の命を得るためである。

ARABIC

لأنه هكذا أحب الله العالم حتى بذل ابنه الوحيد لكي لا يهلك كل من يؤمن به بل تكون له الحياة الأبدية.

FRENCH

Car Dieu a tant aimé le monde qu'il a donné son Fils unique, afin que quiconque croit en lui ne périsse point, mais qu'il ait la vie éternelle.

SPANISH

Porque de tal manera amó Dios al mundo, que ha dado a su Hijo unigénito, para que todo aquel que en él cree, no se pierda, mas tenga vida eterna.

THAI

เพราะว่า พระเจ้าทรงรักโลก, จนได้ประทานพระบุตร องค์เดียวของ พระองค์, เพื่อทุกคนที่วางใจในพระบุตรนั้น จะมิได้พินาศ, แต่มีชีวิตนิรันดร์.

HINDI

क्योंकि परमेश्वर ने जगत से ऐसा प्रेम रखा कि उस ने अपना एकलौता पुत्र दे दिया, ताकि जो कोई उस पर विश्वास करे, वह नाश न हो, परन्तु अनन्त जीवन पाए।

RUSSIAN

Ибо так возлюбил Бог мир, что отдал Сына Своего единородного, дабы всякий, верующий в Него, не погиб, но имел жизнь вечную.

have been translations since the days of Martin Luther and Tyndale. In other languages translations have been made only recently. And every year translations are made into yet other languages.

The words of the Bible have been translated into more languages than any other words in the world. It is being translated into additional languages every year. Nobody knows for sure into how many different languages the Bible has now been translated. Some peoples even today have no written language. Teachers translate the words of parts of the Bible into the language of the people, and the people memorize these words. Then they teach the words to others. Sometimes few outsiders ever know that this translation has been made.

In the case of some other people, a written language was created and taught so that the Bible could be translated and read. So no one knows for sure exactly into how many languages and dialects portions of the Bible have been translated around the world.

The American Bible Society reports that parts of the Bible have been translated into more than twelve hundred languages. The whole Bible has been translated into 236 languages. The words of the Bible are the only words which so many people can read, each in his own language.

Some of the translations are in languages which are used by only a few people, and so only a few copies are made. For example, it is reported that a translation was made into Arawak for use by a small language group in British Guiana. In Nigeria a language called Bachama is used in a part of the country, and parts of the New Testament have been made for the people who speak this language. So it has been with many languages.

In other languages which are written and spoken by large numbers of people, like Chinese or Japanese or German or French or Spanish or Italian, millions of copies of the Bible have been published and distributed to people who want them.

≫≫≫≫≫ The Bible in Many Languages ≪≪≪≪≪

Number of languages into which entire Bible has been translated: 236

Number of languages into which the entire New Testament has been translated: 297

Number of languages into which at least one book has been translated: 1232

During 1964 complete Bibles were published for the first time in five languages, and portions were published for the first time in twenty-four languages.

The Bible World Today

NO one knows exactly where or under what circumstances each one of the books in the Bible was written. Often we wish that those who first put the material in the Bible into writing had put down a date and an address and then signed it as we do when we publish a book today! But men of old thought what was being written was important because God wanted it written. When and where and by whom it was written down was not considered important.

In some of the books places and names are given which help the scholars know when and where the book was written. In others there is very little written-in information.

The Bible Lands

The scholars do know that all the books of the Bible were written in that part of the world which lies between what is now the Caspian Sea and the Persian Gulf on the east, and on across the Mediterranean Sea to what is now Italy. All these areas, including part of what is now Egypt and the northern shores of the Mediterranean, are known as the Bible lands. But the land just east of the Mediterranean Sea is what is usually called the "Holy Land."

These are the lands of which the Bible tells, and in these lands the people of its pages lived and its books were put into writing, century after century.

These are ancient lands. They have seen many nations rise and fall through the centuries. They are very real lands. You can find them on your map, though they have new names today.

It is in these lands that the ancient patriarchs lived; it is here that Moses led the people; it is here that David ruled; it is here that the great prophets spoke for God; it is here that Jesus lived and taught and was put to death; it is here that the disciples so courageously proclaimed the good news that Jesus was alive; it was from here that Paul, the great missionary, traveled into the Gentile world to tell the people about Jesus; and it was here that the mighty acts of God to his people as proclaimed by poets and prophets were first put into writing.

Because all these important events in human history took place in these lands, people from all over the world want to go there. They want to walk where the patriarchs and the prophets and Jesus and the disciples walked. They want to see the waters and the hills that they saw. It makes all that the Bible says seem more real to visit the lands where it all took place.

Bible Places
on Present-Day Maps

There is very little left today of the cities or the buildings that the people of Bible times knew. Generation after generation has passed. Wind and water and heat and cold have passed

over them. Wars have wrought destruction, over and over. Cities have been destroyed, then new cities built on the ruins, and these in turn have been destroyed as the long ages rolled slowly by. At the site on the Jordan River called Jericho, the men who study the ruins say that at least seven different cities have been built and destroyed there. Another modern city stands on this site today.

There is a modern city of Jerusalem, too. It is high on a hill, as it was in the days of King David, but the buildings of David's day are gone. There is a large rock, called the Dome of the Rock, on which stood the great Temple which Solomon built. But instead of the Temple, a Moslem mosque stands there today. Jerusalem is now a divided city; part of it is in the state of Israel and part of it in the Arab state of Jordan. Few things remain to be seen that were there in the time of Jesus. But nearby is the

A view of the older portion of Jerusalem, showing the Temple area and a corner of the city wall.

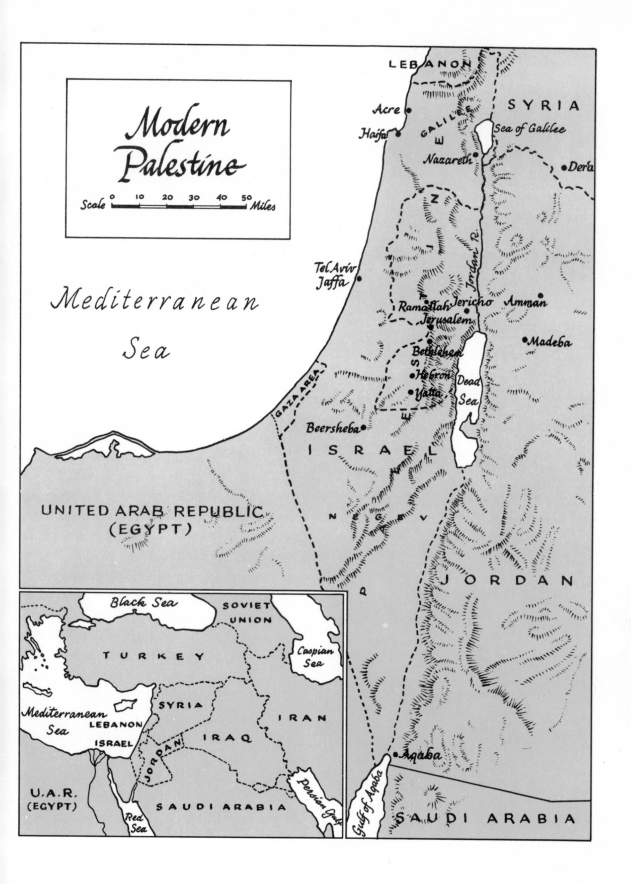

Modern
Palestine

Scale 0 10 20 30 40 50 Miles

Mediterranean

Sea

LEBANON

Acre

Haifa

GALILEE

Sea of Galilee

Nazareth

Derʿa

SYRIA

Tel Aviv
Jaffa

Ramallah
Jerusalem

Jericho

Amman

Jordan R.

Madeba

Bethlehem

Hebron

Yatta

Dead
Sea

Beersheba

ISRAEL

GAZA AREA

UNITED ARAB REPUBLIC
(EGYPT)

NEGEV

JORDAN

Aqaba

Gulf of Aqaba

SAUDI ARABIA

Black Sea

SOVIET
UNION

TURKEY

Caspian
Sea

Mediterranean
Sea

SYRIA

LEBANON

IRAQ

IRAN

ISRAEL

JORDAN

U.A.R.
(EGYPT)

Red
Sea

SAUDI ARABIA

Persian Gulf

Garden of Gethsemane where Jesus prayed.

The Sea of Galilee is there, too, along the shores of which Jesus taught, and the Jordan River still flows into the Dead Sea. Bethlehem and Nazareth, where Jesus was born and where he grew up, are there, though they are not like they were when Jesus was a child.

In the cities along the Mediterranean Sea where Paul traveled and taught and organized little churches, there are reminders of the great missionary. Many of the cities which Paul visited have been destroyed by war, and new cities have been built on some sites. Rome still endures, of course, though a different Rome from the one of Paul's day. Only a few ancient ruins from Paul's time may be seen.

So though the nation and cities change, the lands of the Bible are real lands and they are still on the maps.

Israel Today

But there is strife today in these lands. The new state of Israel is a Jewish state. Israel to-

A view of Nazareth from the east.

Older part of Bethlehem, seen from the southwest.

day is a small but vigorous state, a strip along the eastern shore of the Mediterranean Sea. East and south of Israel are Arab states. The Arabs do not recognize Israel as a state, and do not want it to continue. They think it was set up unfairly. The people of Israel think this is their homeland, the land of their fathers. Israel is determined to preserve its nationhood. So there is tension. Both trade and travel are restricted between Israel and the Arab states, and often fighting flares up along the borders. The United Nations is trying hard to keep the peace and to work out some agreements. But it is proving a very hard problem to solve.

It is sad that in the lands of the Bible there should be today such serious differences among the peoples.

Yet thousands of visitors go there every year. Thousands of people from all over the world consider this land to be indeed the Holy Land.

The Archaeologists at Work

Sometimes it is not easy for the scholars to find out just where the ancient places referred to in the Bible belong on a present-day map. But they are learning more and more about it all the time. Archaeologists dig down into the ground and find, covered by the centuries, exciting evidences of the life in the ancient places about which the Bible tells.

Sometimes a little hill turns out to be a great buried city of the ancient Bible world. Carefully the archaeologists clear away the earth, layer after layer. They find remains of palaces and waterworks and walls and cemeteries. They find many of the things mentioned in the Bible which have long been buried. For example, they have found Solomon's famous horse stables at Megiddo (I KINGS 9:15, 17–19).

Sometimes what these seeking scholars find is an ancient library which contains old manuscripts of the Bible. During very recent years some manuscripts have been found of both the Old Testament and the New Testament books, much nearer to the first manuscripts than any previously known. It is testimony to the faithfulness and care and devotion of the copyists through the generations that these older copies prove how few copying errors have been made.

The Dead Sea Scrolls

The most famous recent "find" of ancient manuscripts are the Dead Sea Scrolls. In 1947 some Bedouin goat herders, looking for a lost goat, went into a cave near the Dead Sea. They found some strange-looking bundles. These bundles proved to be very important. They

Excavations showing the ruins of ancient Jericho, one of the oldest cities of the Bible world.

turned out to be ancient manuscripts. When they were carefully unwrapped by scholars, the manuscripts were found to be among the most important discoveries in centuries. A manuscript in Hebrew of the book of Isaiah is hundreds of years older than any other Hebrew manuscript in existence, and so nearer to the original writings.

Libraries and museums are taking care of these manuscripts. Scholars are learning how to treat the ancient material of the books so it can be separated without crumbling. Many of these scrolls have now been translated, and what the scholars have read in these ancient manuscripts have made clearer the meaning of some parts of the Bible.

Right now the lands of the Bible are being searched for more and more old manuscripts and more and more facts about Bible times. The archaeologists are helping us to know more and more about the life and times of the Bible people and about the Bible places. Maybe the papers tomorrow will have news of another important find!

(a)   *(b)*

(a) Ruins of the Qumram settlement near the Dead Sea, the desolate area where the Dead Sea scrolls were found in caves. (b) The scrolls were discovered stored in jars like these, which had preserved them for centuries.

A copper scroll found at Qumram, recording where national treasures were hidden.

God, All the People, and the Bible

"IN THE beginning, God!" The Bible began in the plan of God to make himself known to man.

Through the ages men responded to God. There were the men back at the beginning, before there was any writing, who listened and responded and told others; the men who listened and wrote down what they understood; the men who brought together the writings of earlier men and organized them into rolls of Scripture. There were the men who suffered and died to preserve it and make it known. Then there were all the men who copied so faithfully, generation after generation, the sacred text so it would be preserved. And the men who translated it into the new languages the people were speaking.

There were the men who used printing to make the Bible easily available. There were the men who taught others to read so they could know for themselves what the Bible says. There were the men who, year after year, studied the words and made new translations to keep up with the changes in languages.

Today there are the men who are working so hard to uncover ancient cities to find out more and more about the events of which the Bible tells so they can help people understand better what the ancient book says to men. There are those who are finding and translating more ancient manuscripts. There are those who are making new translations in many more languages all around the world.

In our own country today there are the men and women who study together in the colleges and universities to learn more and more about what the Bible says. And in your own home town there are the men and women who preach in the churches and teach boys and girls to help people today to understand its message. And in many of the great countries of the world, what the Bible says is deep in the roots of the nation's laws and its life.

The Bible also speaks to the need of each person wherever he lives, and in his own time in history—yesterday, today, tomorrow.

ABOUT THE AUTHOR

MARY ALICE JONES, author of the famous *"Tell Me"* books and many other publications, is one of the most highly regarded authorities in the field of religious education. Parents, teachers, and young people all testify to the broad appeal of her writings.

Born in Dallas, Texas, Miss Jones has already crowded two or three lifetimes of work into her career. She took her B.A. degree at the University of Texas, and later took an M.A. degree at Northwestern University and a Ph.D. at Yale Divinity School. She has long been active in the field of religious education. For many years she was Director of Children's work for the International Council of Religious Education, and more recently was Director of the Department of Christian Education of Children for the Methodist Church. She has supervised laboratory summer schools for children, taught at both Yale and Northwestern universities, lectured at literally scores of other universities and colleges, served on various national committees and conferences, including two White House Conferences, and has contributed to many educational publications.

In addition to these activities, Miss Jones has found time to write and edit more than thirty books dealing with religious education for children. Best known of these, perhaps, is her series of *"Tell Me"* books: TELL ME ABOUT GOD, TELL ME ABOUT JESUS, TELL ME ABOUT HEAVEN, TELL ME ABOUT THE BIBLE, TELL ME ABOUT PRAYER, TELL ME ABOUT CHRISTMAS, and TELL ME ABOUT GOD'S PLAN FOR ME. Her books have been translated into many languages, including Japanese, East Indian, and African dialects.

PRINTED IN U.S.A.